What Color Is The Wind?

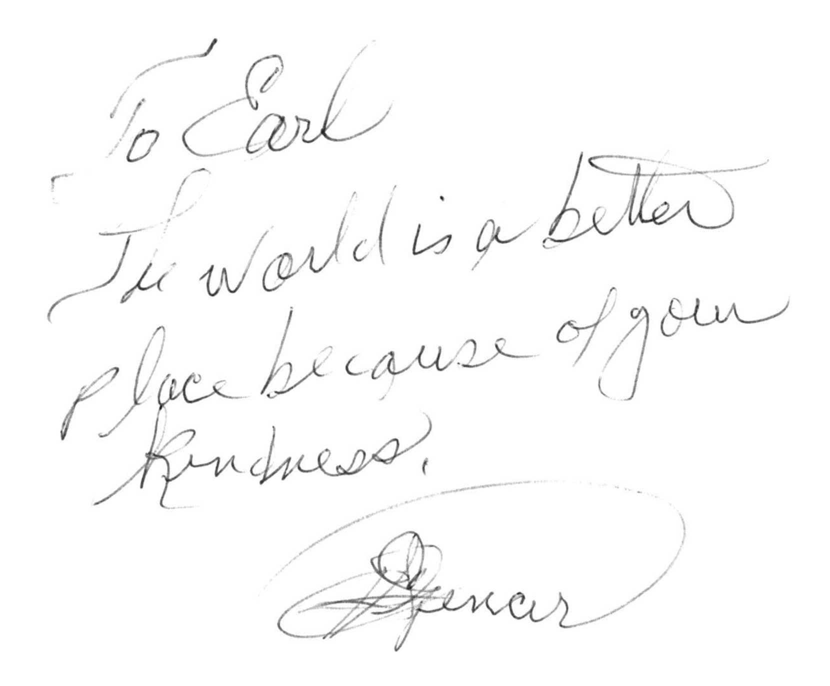

Edna P. Spencer

outskirtspress
DENVER, COLORADO

What Color Is The Wind?

v2.0

Outskirts Press, Inc.
http://www.outskirtspress.com

ISBN: 978-1-4327-9378-4

PRINTED IN THE UNITED STATES OF AMERICA

In Memory of my daughter
Olivia Rochelle Spencer
My little Shelly

Acknowledgements

For her endless patience and for all that she has shared with me and taught me, a sincere thank you to Ruth H. Jacobs, PhD. Her guidance helped me to step back and take a broader look at my experiences, and so doing, gather the courage to probe deeper, and put in writing things that have nor been spoken of. I wish to thank Gary Overvold. PhD, for giving me such valuable counsel and support. A heart felt thank you to Margaret LeRoux for her editing, recommendations, and contagious excitement. Finally, to the one who always says you can, when I begin to think that I can't, to my husband, Cornelius B. Spencer, my friend, companion, and lover.

JARRETT FAMILY GENEALOGICAL CHART

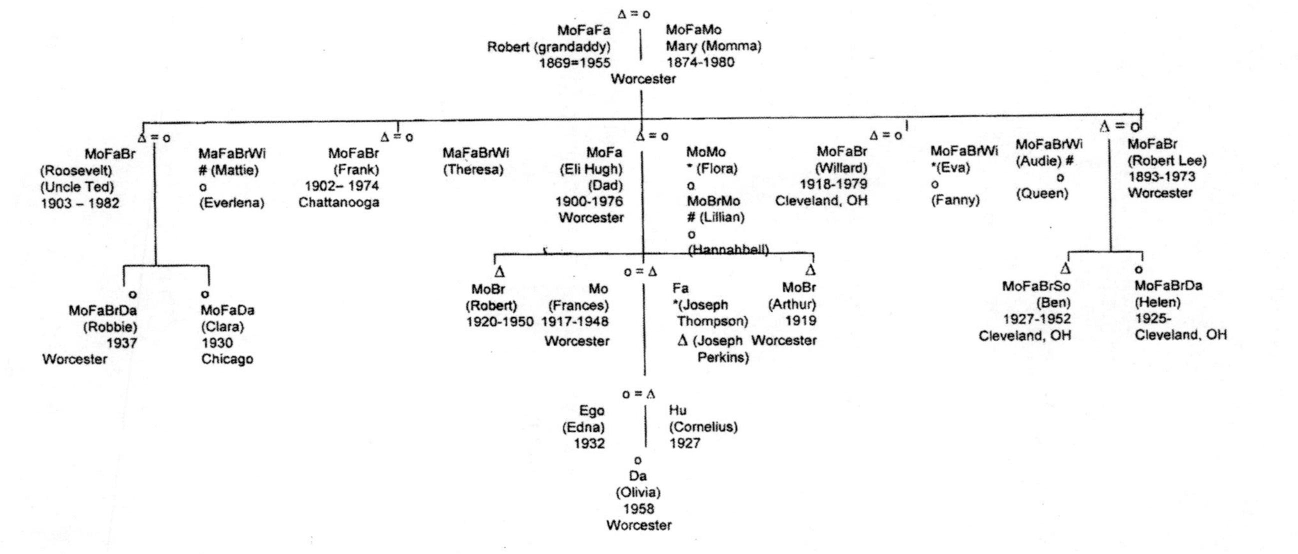

Diagram of Jarrett Family Kinship showing the consanguine and affinal ties of kinship from the perspective of Edna P. Thompson (Ego) daughter of Frances (Jarrett) Thompson and Joseph Thompson.

Δ - Male
o -Female
*- Death
- Divorce
Mo-Mother
Fa - Father

Br – Brother
Hu – Husband
Wi – Wife
Da – Daughter
So – Son

Table of Contents

A restless ocean stirs many emotions to the surface, as though the wildness of it is contagious. Wildness frees the spirit and causes the body to temporarily discard its tensions. But all days must end and it is time for us to take our leave. I stand and take one final look into eternity. I am of the eighth generation of my family on this continent. Over two hundred years ago my forefathers also stood somewhere along this Atlantic coast, they also turned for a final look into the face of a dying hope, then faced the land and walked into a living hell.

Introduction

FREQUENTLY, THE DECISIONS that have the greatest impact on how we live our lives are made by others.

While the event of my birth was being recorded at Chattanooga City Hospital, American socialism was experiencing the convulsive jerks and tremors that usually precede death. As a result of some of those events, historians have recorded that time as a period of one of the greatest crises in American history. It was the four-month period from November 1932 to March 4, 1933, the date of Franklin Delano Roosevelt's Presidential Inauguration—the brief period between Hoover's defeat and Roosevelt's ascent to power. For Afro Americans, it was neither a defeat nor a victory. Roosevelt's remedy for the country's ills was a new deal for the people—a program of economic and social welfare legislation. Regionalism was conceived, under the new deal umbrella. Regionalism would develop the natural resources, dam the rivers, secure the topsoil and uproot the people.

Nancy Grant describes Regionalism as a means for the South to preserve its unique character. The South's economy had an agricultural base, it fostered a rural life style, and its society was based on racial segregation. When administered by southern controlled regional planners, the philosophy of regionalism fit and preserved this southern caste system, almost without adjustment. The fact that regionalism was government funded made no difference. The planners, who were sometimes referred to as the fathers of the Tennessee Valley Association, were Kenneth D. McKeller and George W. Norris. They organized the Association in 1933. They decided to retire poor farm land and develop the natural resources of the Tennessee River drainage basin and its adjoining territory. The people of the Valley, it is said, were promised a new era; they accepted and believed the promise. This decision would eventually change my family's way of life forever.

During this time of depression, some (those without political power) were more depressed than others. Although blacks represented a large segment of the population, they were the powerless group, and they soon discovered that the depression did not mean an equalization of suffering. Instead, blacks found themselves becoming more depressed as the energy of the nation became re-directed from a quest for material gain to a singular struggle for survival. Stress pushed attitudes to the surface in areas that had previously shielded them behind a subtle facade of liberalism. In Massachusetts, for example, the state that would become home for my family, the unemployment rates for early 1937 were recorded as 23.2 percent for blacks and 15.7 percent for whites.

Assuming that the black population was undercounted and that these statistics excluded agricultural occupations, the statistics were low. An accurate count that included all occupations would have resulted in higher statistics for both blacks and whites. However, there would have remained a disproportionate difference between the groups. This disparity still continues to come to light during times when the nation experiences economic problems, and even in relatively prosperous times.

The Jarrett family was more fortunate than some. My great grandfather's farm was small, but it was a very rich piece of bottomland that produced more than enough vegetables and fruits to sustain us. My grandfather and one of his brothers left the farm in the 20's and migrated to the Philadelphia steel mills. However, as the nation's economy worsened, whites began to encroach on blacks in the undesirable, unskilled occupations. This happened even in the service occupations that were heretofore considered to be below the status of any white individual, even the poorest. Most were domestic occupations that had been done first by slaves and maintained the stigma of slavery, I believe, to some extent even to this day. This situation resulted in my grandfather and his brother losing their jobs in Philadelphia and moving to an unheard of town in Massachusetts called Worcester. They would have gone on to Boston, if there had been a chance of finding work there. This initial migration was to result in the permanent relocation of our family. After my father's death in 1935, my mother also came to Massachusetts. I have not been able to determine the exact date of her arrival here. Roosevelt (Ted) was the last of my grand-uncles to work the farm with his father. He remained with his parents, or they with him, until their deaths. The youngest Jarrett son, Willard, was unmarried in those days, and traveled about the country finding work wherever he could.

My great grandfather was always granddaddy to the children in the family and great grandmother was Momma to everyone.

Farmers also need money; children who had migrated sent money "home" whenever they could. Uncle Ted worked for a while for the TVA. But jobs for blacks were very limited.

The TVA did not begin to desegregate until the middle of the 1950's. There was no section for blacks in the plans to improve the Valley. Staff memoranda on Negro Employment in the TVA, record the low percentage of black employment, and the wage differentials that resulted in blacks being paid as little as one third the hourly rate paid to whites.

Construction of the TVA dams began in 1933 and lasted for more than a decade. To prevent flooding of the Tennessee River, they flooded our Valley and eventually our fertile little farm also succumbed to the water. The land made available to the small, displaced farmers was so inferior that many could no longer make a living farming. Some even found it difficult to raise enough food to sustain their families. My grandfather relocated to the Summit on a knoll of hard red clay. I remember watching him plow one summer, after I returned to Tennessee.

The earth was so hard and packed that the mule seemed barely able to pull the blade through it. It wasn't like the rich black earth that rolled smoothly back from the plow in Tyner. That was earth that opened to reveal and give life; this was stagnant and dead.

It's ironic that the thing that many of the inhabitants of the Valley cherished most was the thing that made the Valley so attractive to the Federal Government. That was its remoteness—its peculiar isolation. Until now, I always believed that the isolation was cherished only by the black inhabitants of the Valley. However, studies that have been made of Oakridge citizens mention the peculiar isolation and the significance of it to the poor whites of the Valley who, because they were Oakridgers, were easily identified outside of their own realm.

White Oakridgers frequently found themselves ostracized by whites from other areas of the state.

Another decision. Oakridge would become the location for a nuclear plant. Because of its isolation, the rest of the nation would not be aware of, nor would they be concerned about, the activities that occurred there. If local citizens did become aware of what was being done, they certainly would not understand. Moreover, the location was naturally protected by distance from enemy ships that might attack the coast. The posted fences must have seemed like the final seal on a declaration that said they (the farmers) could never return. In 1942, Oakridge was selected as the site of a plant for the production of the atomic bomb.

That same isolation protected my family from some of the pain of living in a segregated society. In retrospect, we were somewhat like children who cover their eyes and think that they cannot be seen in the darkness. During the first six years of my life, I visited Chattanooga twice; the first trip was during the Christmas season. Momma and I had our pictures taken. Uncle Frank, one of my grandfather's brothers, took me on my second trip. My only other contact (if those trips can be called contact) with whites resulted from an occasional walk to a country store that was a mile or so away from our farm. Also, once each year, a small band of gypsies traveled through the area. Ben and I saw them from a distance. Having been told all of the ridiculous stories that have been conjured up about gypsies, we were sure that we would be stolen or placed under some horrible magic spell if we spoke to them or got too close. I never remember a white person entering our house, or standing on our porch. For those unfamiliar with southern custom, this statement may seem strange. However, it was customary for white insurance agents to have a seat on the porch when collecting the twenty-five and fifty cents for premiums. It was not unusual for the agent to ask

"Aunty" for a drink of water. My great grandfather would not allow this. The only words exchanged were those that were absolutely necessary to transact business. How did my great grandfather get away with such things? Momma used to tell us about the time when he organized a group of black men in the Valley. Armed with shotguns, the men stood guard around the jail all night to keep another black from being lynched. Of course, the whites did finally lynch him under the guise of the courts. Great Granddaddy had many adventures. He was permitted to live because, in spite of his stubbornness, he posed no threat to the ruling elite. His interest did not extend beyond the people of the Valley. Instead of killing him, they simply said that his accident left him a little crazy. The accident occurred when he was working as a helper with a line crew. Someone, accidentally or deliberately, dropped a wrench from the top of a line pole. The wrench struck almost directly in the center of the top of his skull. Momma always became angry when she told us the story because they (the whites) didn't bother to take him to a doctor. A lesser man would have died on the spot. But Granddaddy lived, and in spite of the fact that there was a noticeable dent in his skull the size of a quarter and a fourth of an inch in depth, he was never insane, although he was plagued by severe headaches in his later years.

During those early years of life, my nurturing was for independence and self-worth and that nurturing was not undermined by exposure to the "colored only" signs or the verbal and physical abuse that is very much a part of a segregated society. However, I must point out that there were white as well as black inhabitants of the Valley. Most of us were poor, and though there was no public camaraderie between the races, there was a kind of mutual caring. I can remember my great grandmother going to a white family's home and taking her turn sitting with their sick mother. Just as I remember hearing her and Granddaddy talking about a white woman sitting with a very ill black neighbor. Outsiders would have some difficulty with this. It's best understood when you realize that there were good people in that Valley, and they came in more than one color.

As surely as this strange isolation supported a feeling of self—worth, it shielded me against the experiences that would have taught me to deal effectively with bigotry. I moved to Massachusetts in 1938 totally unprepared. I had been shielded against the prerequisite for survival.

> "Bigotry is a burden to everyone, black and white, in America. But, it is a personal burden to the Negro — a burden of shame and outrage imposed on him at the earliest moment of consciousness and never lifted till death, and all his energies, mental, emotional, spiritual must be held in reserve for carrying it."[1]

The dams of the TVA drew closer to Black Oakridge and the church continued to be the nucleus of our social activities. At least one half of each Sunday was spent in church. Picnics and suppers were held at the church and even funerals were an all day social event, although I never heard of wakes before coming to Massachusetts. Belonging to church and family provides support; the reward of belonging creates an almost unwavering commitment to the church and/or the family.

I mentioned that black Americans simply became more

---

1 J. Saunders Redding, On Being Negro In America. New York: Howard W. Sams & Co., Inc., 1951, P.152.

depressed during the Depression, yet they clung to their beliefs and their heroes. When Mussolini's troops invaded Ethiopia in 1935, people knew where their pennies in the mission collection plate would go. And when the Lion of Juda was forced to leave the land of Solomon in May 1936, the prayers and the pennies, that could be spared, increased. Ethiopia was after all a black nation; its defeat would bring pain; it would have been a defeat to all blacks. I remember hearing the adults discuss Ethiopia's fate and express the despair and frustration in those discussions. This was also the time when Communism was ardently courting black Americans, especially those who were well educated and/or professional. But their success in courting was limited. Afro Americans were not swayed by the courtship's promises. Instead, they merged their hopes in their heroes. Haile Selassie was one of those heroes. Joe Louis, Jesse Owens and Marion Anderson were among these heroes.

Wars have always resulted in major changes for Afro Americans. The Civil War, World War I and World War II all resulted in a multitude of changes. One of the most interesting phenomenons was the black migration that occurred between the two world wars. It is referred to as the largest mass migration in the history of the United States. Pushed, as though by the prevailing winds, it was a massive wave of flesh from the rural South into the industrial, urban North. It was the use, by a people, of one of the few freedoms available to them. The freedom to move and seek, hoping to find the jobs that paid the "good money". The TVA did not alter the flow of black migration from Tennessee.

> "The Atomic Energy Commission, an agency that had a reputation for a concern for advancing human welfare, blatantly violated any reasonable standard of equal

opportunity by hiring fewer than 4 percent blacks in its 37,000 Oakridge work force. Moreover, the largest proportions of those hired were common laborers."[2]

A further indication of how well regionalism served to perpetuate the cast system. But, life cannot be all sickness for those who survive. It is their ability to maintain an inner joy, a hope that always lingers very close to the surface of the psyche ready to spring forth with the slightest prodding. That is why we are survivors. Edward E. Wilson describes that inner joy beautifully in his essay "The Joys of Being A Negro."

> "An idea has unfortunately gotten abroad that being a Negro is like being in solitary confinement—away from the rest of the World. It is thought, indeed, that there could be no place chosen so gloomy or so hopeless in which to be born as among this race composed to some extent of descendants of Ham. Yet the whole question depends—all other things do in life—on the point of view and the state of mind. —Life's happiness lies in anticipation. It *is* a truism that perfectly fits the Negro's case. So much lies before him, the things he can hope to achieve are so much more numerous than those, which Aryans can look forward to, that his pleasures of hope are endless—why seek disillusion in attainment? It is but seldom that delights grow stale by being transformed from the imaginary to the real."[3]

---

2 [2]Nancy Grant, "Blacks, Regional Planning, and the TVA" (PhD dissertation, The University of Chicago 1978), P.123.

3 [3]E.E. Wilson, "The Joys of Being A Negro, Essay. June Sochen, The Black Man and the American Dream, P.265.

Yet, the total isolation scenario has also much sadness. We are end products of the events that preceded us. A race encumbered by a hundred years of isolation in and irrelevance to the society that surrounds it develops expertise at outsideness of isolation. We have learned the total meaning of making the supreme effort without receiving logical results. We have tasted the bitterness of being without effect.

Tennessee is a peculiar state, unlike other southern states. At the onset of the Civil War, there were 7,300 freedmen living in Tennessee.

My great grandfather was the son of one of those freedmen. There were also 275,719 slaves. The state seemed to vacillate between its liberal and conservative policies. It must be pointed out that the Ku Klux Klan also originated in Tennessee—in Pulaski in 1865.

And so these events impacted on the members of our family and one by one the children, grandchildren and great grandchildren of Robert and Mary Jarrett added their bodies to the great black migratory wave. There was one exception. The last to leave Tennessee were my great grandparents. They arrived in Worcester, Massachusetts in 1941. Frank, their eldest son, lived out his life in the state of the Iris and the mockingbird. He could never leave home.

CHAPTER I

Hogs Can See the Wind

OUR HOUSE SAT on the side of a gently sloped, lushly forested hill. The fields, where Granddaddy, my great grandfather and Uncle Ted plowed and planted, were broad, natural plateaus that cut into the side of the hill. Walking up the main road from Chattanooga, you became aware of the diversity of the area as you passed banks of bright red clay pierced by honeybee tunnels, and then thick wooded areas of pine, hickory, walnut, cedar and birch. And, always honey suckle and other bushes grew along the perimeter, creating a natural fence of fragrance that coaxed trespassers in rather than keeping them out. Around a bend in the road, the first plateau might surprise a traveler, because suddenly there were two houses, one on either side of an open yard. To the right was a small, but new bungalow, white shingled and painted. To the left was our house. It rested against the side of the hill like a huge piece of slate grey drift wood that had been washed, sanded, and faded by sun and ocean for countless numbers of years, then cast, by some phantom wave, against the side of this hill where it almost seemed to hide under the canopy of trees. As if it was in fear of being found and put adrift again.

Under no circumstance do I mean to imply that this little driftwood house was without design or the kind of character that inanimate objects acquire after being used and/or occupied by humans for a while. This four—room structure sported both front and back piazzas. The cistern was at the far end of the back porch near my bedroom window. During spring and summer, roses and irises grew in a profusion of color along the front walk leading to the barn, the meat house and the outhouse. The irises had spread along both sides of the path and a few could be seen going towards the road. The back door opened directly into the kitchen. My room was to the right and directly across was the room shared by Uncle Ted and Ben and, finally, there was the front bedroom that was a bit larger than the others. This was Granddaddy and Momma's room; its furnishings consisted of a large brass bed, a chest of drawers, a dome top trunk for storing quilt fabric for future products and other special items. Momma used to put a handful of walnuts in each year when she washed and stored the quilts. The nuts were used like cedar to make the trunk smell good. The most important feature of that room was its fireplace. Granddaddy's chair sat directly in front of it. That fireplace was the family's evening gathering place.

In the early 1930's technology had not reached the small farmers. Or, perhaps I should say that the small farmer did not have the means to reach technology. Mules still played a crucial role in the farmers' survival. Granddaddy's stock always consisted of a mule, one cow, sometimes with a calf, and two hogs. I remember that whenever the wind would begin to rise, signaling an approaching storm, the hogs would go into a frenzy of squealing, running and biting each other. Granddaddy would look up at the sky and say, "Storms a coming" in that way that he had of seeming to be talking to himself. "Them hogs can see the wind." Once I asked him, "What color is the wind Granddaddy?" As he wired the meat house door shut, he answered, "Red-it's red."

This was my beginning with all of the harshness and softness that is part of farm life where birth and death are almost daily events, and the quality of one's life fluctuates, depending on the seasons of good years and bad years. Many things can be said for such beginnings. Had it not been for the resiliency that I developed early in life, I would never have survived. And, without the first joy, I would not have found so much satisfaction in the living and growing process.

Until my sixth year, my world was confined within the boundaries of that small farm. I shared that world with my great grandparents, my grand uncle, Ted, and my cousin, Ben. For me, it was as warm and secure as any home could be. Children who are loved are never poor. Only the adults struggled and concerned themselves with survival. Ben and I filled our days with other things. We shared happiness and pain; he was my hero, protector and friend. Ours was a friendship nurtured by the kind of unquestioning mutual trust that only children have.

Tennessee's winters are as damp as its summers. The humidity doesn't disseminate and vanish with the cold, as one would expect. Instead, it seems to intensify, becoming heavier and sharpened by the cold. It penetrates the skin and chills the bones. It is a foe with which to reckon. Thus, sounds of early winter mornings in the Jarrett household revealed an unvarying ritual to overcome, or at least, survive the reckoning.

Spontaneously, the rooster, the Big Ben and Granddaddy seemed to come to life. Granddaddy was always the first member of the household to rise. Nothing deterred him; I don't recall him ever missing a morning, not even for illness.

Even now, if I close my eyes, I can hear him and conjure images of those mornings. He coughed, pulled on his trousers, followed by shoes and socks; then he went into the middle room to wake up the fire in the big pot bellied heater. Our main source of heat, the big heater, was banked at night with chunks of coal to reduce its oxygen supply just enough to keep the bottom coals smoldering, but not enough to allow a flaming combustion that would devour the coals. Granddaddy would shake the grate clearing it of ashes and permitting oxygen to enter. As the coals began to glow a bright red, he piled on wood and fresh coal.

In minutes, I could hear the wood crackling and popping like kernels of corn, and the fragrance of burning wood joined the pungent coal dust, sending a promise of warmth through the house. Our winter coal supply was provided compliments of the railroad, through one of its unplanned public benefits. Momma, Ben and I walked the tracks and gathered the pieces that fell from passing freights.

While the big heater slowly developed a crimson belt around its belly, Granddaddy went to the kitchen to continue his chores. The next sound would be that of the stove iron as he lifted the heavy iron lids from the kitchen stove. Its grates also had to be cleared of yesterday's residue of ashes, before a new fire could be started. He searched through the kindling box, picking out the smallest of the translucent honey amber splinters. Sometimes I could hear him snap pieces of wood to make them smaller before stacking them teepee fashion, over newspaper that had been crumbled and placed on the grate with hickory and whatever else was available. Southern pine is so rich in rosin that it burns, when exposed to flame, almost as rapidly as paper, and its melting rosin is like kerosene in the firebed. The smell of burning pine is still pleasant to me.

By now, Momma was up and she and Granddaddy would talk briefly. Then while she washed and dressed, he would go out to milk, feed and water the animals. This is when I would frequently drift back into the warmth of sleep. My second awakening was to the sound of Momma calling and the smell of ham or bacon sizzling in the black iron skillet, coffee perking and biscuits baking. In those days on a farm, meals were prepared and served at specific times. And all family members ate at those times, because there was no way to keep food uniformly warm or cold for latecomers. Momma always managed to get Ben and me out of bed, washed, dressed and seated at the table just at the moment when she took the biscuits out of the oven and was ready to put breakfast, steaming hot, before us. Somehow everything became cooked at the same time. No biscuits have ever equaled Momma's.

For the men, some seasons on the farm were busier than others. For Momma that was never the case. There was no end to her chores. She continuously cooked, washed, quilted and mended, bodies as well as clothing. The floors and walls of that old house had been scrubbed so often with her homemade lye soap, that its interior was the same driftwood grey as its outer walls. She also helped care for the farm animals usually doing the evening milking.

Born, Mary Moore, Momma was small, fair, and had blue/grey eyes. The daughter of slaves, she was one of a large number of children, there were nine in all. She often told us how lucky she was not to have been born any earlier. We never knew the exact date of her birth. However, since the Emancipation Proclamation was issued by Abraham Lincoln effective January 1, 1863, I assume that she must have been born at some time during the following two or three years—close enough to have been impacted by the fact of slavery almost as much as she would have been had she been branded. Unfortunately, Momma did not tell us all of the stories of slavery that her elders had told her. She had command of the survival mechanism that many of the newly free or barely free Negroes had adopted: Don't fret; "the meek shall inherit the world" or, if not, one must not covet anything on earth, because our rewards will be in heaven.

Momma's nurturing and life experiences had left her with the kind of a submissiveness that one develops after prolonged exposure to stress over which one has no control. I say resembles, because she was not totally submissive and, in fact, would take a stand against anyone who bothered her children or grandchildren. She possessed a quiet determination that usually won her battles. She did tell us about Poppa, her father, as that required an explanation. Whenever any of the children saw the Moore family portrait, the first question was "Who is the white man?" Great, Great Grandfather's hair was silver, and his beard reached midway of his chest; he was the plantation master's son. And, his black heritage was only apparent in the slight curliness of his hair. His children were a bit better, although Momma had blue/grey eyes. Most of them had light brown or amber colored eyes, and their skin began to show the promise of brown. It seems that Moore (the master of the planation) beat and raped Poppa's mother one Sunday morning when she had stayed home from church because she was ill. In spite of the beating, great, great grandmother jumped out of a window in an attempt to get away from Moore. And that was when he broke her arm to instill in her mind the fact that he was master. There were other stories, e.g., brandings on the most sensitive areas of the body. Slaves would sometimes be branded on their foreheads. The agony of the disfigurement was a constant reminder of the agony of the iron.

Momma used to hum as she went about her daily chores. Her favorite hymn was "Precious Lord", and that was what she usually hummed or sang very softly as if singing to herself. She married my great grandfather when she wasn't much more than a girl. As I mentioned earlier, the stories of slave experiences had been handed down to her by her parents, who were former slaves. However, she and Granddaddy had lived through the turn of the century. They were members of the disfranchised.

Robert Jarrett looked like a pure blooded African. He was a handsome black man. Not exceptionally tall, he was no more than five feet, eleven inches. However, he had a powerful physique, with large hands and arms. Born a freeman, he was always outspoken, even in Tennessee, long before it was popular to do so. He used to preach at the Baptist Church when they were without a regular preacher. Or, he would serve as a substitute when the preacher was away. Frequently, he would call meetings of the men of the church to discuss issues that were affecting or threatening their families. The family also credited Granddaddy with saving Uncle John. It seems that Uncle John chose to end an affair that he had been having with his employer's wife. Uncle John was their chauffeur. With Uncle John passing for white, Granddaddy arranged his passage and some of the men, who worked for the railroad, slipped him into a whites only passenger car headed North. They managed to get him out of Tennessee at night, a few hours in front of the Sheriff and the Klan. It was at least fifteen years before Momma saw Uncle John again. But, he made it and he lived.

No description of Granddaddy would be complete

without mentioning his sense of humor and love of children, all children. His eyes seemed to always sparkle with mischief. He insisted that his sons be men but he tempered his demands with love and understanding. He spoiled his granddaughters.

Momma was the only one who ever called him "Rob". My great grandparents were married for well over 50 years. They were the trunk of our family tree. They bore the blunt of the extended family. For all but two years of their lives together they had children, grandchildren and/or great grandchildren to care for. I never heard them complain. Certainly, Momma would have been justified in complaining or refusing to accept the continuous responsibility.

Our only close neighbors were a young couple in their mid to late thirties. Ben and I always called them Mr. Rubin and Miss Louise. It's still not unusual for southern children to address adults in this manner. We didn't know their last name anyway. Mr. Rubin drove the school bus, a perfect occupation for him, as he loved children and had none of his own. Unlike our driftwood grey, their little bungalow was new, with white shingles and had a trim that I cannot recall. It also had a brick base that gave the illusion of a cellar, and an ornate screen door. Miss Louise did lovely needle crafts that made the little house look like something out of a storybook. Their land abutted ours so that we shared a common yard.

Ben was Robert Lees' son, and my second cousin. Until I was six years old, I thought he was my brother. We had been raised without explanations of circumstances. To describe him, I would say that he was just a boy with no outstanding features or characteristics, except that he inherited Granddaddy's love for mischief, which frequently got him in trouble.

When he wasn't in school or off helping Granddaddy or Uncle Ted, Ben and I were inseparable. My fondest memory of Ben goes back to the Christmas of 1936. That year, his special gift was a shiny red wagon.

He had talked of nothing else the previous summer. The desire to own a red wagon was almost an obsession with him.

Christmas is an exciting time in farm country. It immediately follows the harvest and all those activities involved in harvesting—activities of production to sustain the family during the coming winter months. There is stacking, husking, canning, slaughtering and curing all going on simultaneously. After these chores were finished, Momma would start her holiday baking and Ben and I would make molasses candy or go into the woods with Granddaddy to gather sacks of hickory nuts, black walnuts and sassafras roots for tea. Like squirrels, we filled our cache with all of these marvelous things in anticipation of long winter evenings.

Without a doubt, my great grandfather was one of the greatest storytellers that ever lived. While yams roasted in the coals of the bedroom fireplace, their skins popping and oozing sweetness, we cracked nuts in the belly of a heavy iron frog and munched and listened, while Granddaddy mesmerized us with stories that had been told to previous generations.

"Redhead and Bloody Bones" and "Big Tom" were only two of the characters that I remember. In addition, that was where we heard the stories of the Bible and learned to fear the wrath of God, as well as the fire and brimstone of Hell, in Southern Baptist fashion. There were many times when I went to sleep on the old man's lap in front of that fireplace while its fire crackled and sent dancing shadows, to join those of the kerosene lamp, in an unwritten program of choreography across the wall and ceiling.

So we spent our days and evenings, that December of 1937, until finally, it was Christmas morning. The air was crystal clear and so cold that we could make smoke rings with our breath. Momma had already put us in our long johns with the trap doors. I remember pulling heavy brown stockings over mine. For some reason, I don't recall what my special gift was that year. In our Christmas stockings, we always found an orange, an apple, store bought nuts (pecans) and sometimes even a banana. Granddaddy always bought a giant peppermint cane, and our special gift was usually a small toy. That is why this year was unlike all others, because Ben received the most glorious gift of all. He was nine years old and finally grown up enough to take care of an expensive gift. And there it was under our tree, brighter than the star of Bethlehem. It was the most beautiful red wagon either of us had ever seen—store bought, new and beautiful. This gift would only be equaled, in my eyes, by a very precious book that I would receive the following year. The wagon became the center of conversation. It was a matter of pride that all who entered our house during the holidays had to admire it and comment on how wonderful it was and how lucky Ben was. Only then, could they get on with their visiting.

Ben never was one for school but that winter, his esteem for it was even lower. He could hardly wait to get home. I doubt that he learned very much that year. As quickly as possible after getting home, he would begin to ride. Resting his left knee in the wagon, he would push, scooter fashion, with his right foot and take off lickity-split, a red streak up and down the road, only stopping occasionally to give me a ride, or stopping for supper, when Momma called. In spite of the constant use, the little wagon retained its shiny new look.

At last, the sun's rays began to feel warmer on our cheeks and there were no longer bits of ice floating in the creek.

Spring had arrived, and in a few weeks, school would be over and *Ben* would be home all day. This always made me happy but this year, even more so, we would have a real fun summer coasting down the hill in the wagon. But, the time for the newness of things is short lived and, as summer approached, the novelty of the wagon began to fade. It was not that there was less love for the object. Instead, I think that Ben realized that it was his wagon and that no one would take it from him. In fact, Momma had to begin to remind him to keep the wagon close to the house when he wasn't using it. Mr. Rubin had to drive the school bus into the yard and he might not see the wagon as he turned off the road.

One early spring day, Ben was home from school and was scooting about as usual while I occupied myself playing in my favorite spot beneath the shade tree. When Momma called us to supper, Ben abandoned his vehicle and ran into the house.

Granddaddy had finished saying grace and we were about to start eating when we heard the sickening sound of metal against metal and then, the death crunch. En masse, we rushed to the door. There, beneath the rear right wheel of the school bus, lay all that remained of the little red wagon. Ben looked at his precious wagon while huge silent tears cascaded down his cheeks. My hero wept for his steed, his calico princess wept for him, and Mr. Rubin wept for all of us.

The next winter I started school. We didn't ride the bus. I believe that the bus was used to take the high school students to Booker T. Washington High. The grammar school kids had to walk. Some rode horses. For Ben and me it was about two miles. If the weather was really bad, Granddaddy would hook up the mule and take us to school in the wagon.

Our school was a one-room log structure that had been built by the black men of the Valley. It was located in a thickly forested section of the Valley, as if there was an attempt to hide it from someone. A large pot bellied stove stood in the middle of the room. Where you were seated determined the extent of your warmth during winter months. One side of one's body was usually warm, while the other wise was a bit cooler. The older boys were responsible for keeping the woodpile stocked. Like other rural southern schools, we had one teacher for grades one through eight. I regret that I cannot remember our teacher's name. She may have been one of the finest teachers that I have ever had. With her meager supplies, she taught her students and prepared them to cope with the rigors of high school. She maintained discipline at all times and even developed an athletic program that produced some of the best grammar school runners in our county.

I remember how rapidly I learned to read. The trouble was that there just weren't enough books. I loved to read so much that my special gift the next Christmas was a Little Golden Book titled, Sleeping Beauty. I read that little book so many times that I almost knew it by heart. I still remember the pictures. I gave it special care so as not to soil or damage it in any way. I had no trouble relating to the story. At that tender age, it didn't matter that the prince had blond hair and blue eyes. That book remained unscathed until my six-year-old daughter took possession. It was just too little to compete with the excitement of bigger, more adventurous books, and the excitement of television. So one child's treasure became another child's discarded object. I discovered the excitement of learning during that year in the Oakridge grammar school. It is an excitement that has never left me. Unfortunately, or fortunately, depending on one's perspective, my first year in that school was also my last.

The summer comes up hot in Tennessee. If there is a dry

spell, the red clay turns to a fine powder that coats and seeps into everything. On such a day in August, I looked up from my favorite play area beneath the big shade tree and saw someone walking down the road toward our house.

At first the heat waves caused the figure to shimmer like a reflection on the surface of a lake that had been gently disturbed. As it came closer, the form seemed to solidify and I could soon tell that it was a woman carrying a suitcase. I abandoned my solitary play and ran over to the edge of the yard where the dirt road ended. There I stood, and watched a portrait develop, a portrait that I would remember for the rest of my life.

She was tall, five feet, nine inches to be exact, and thin. Her perfect posture and smooth stride made her appear even taller. She looked almost too fragile to carry the large suitcase. At that moment, I looked directly into her face; she was so pretty. In fact, she was as pretty as the picture of the lady that was in the book that I received last Christmas. She walked right up to me and I stood there looking up into that beautiful face, already sensing an alliance between us.

She put her suitcase down, and placed her hands on my shoulders. With a smile on her face and in her voice, she said, "Edna, don't you remember me?" "I'm your mother." So the adoration commenced and with it, events that would change my life forever.

My mother, Frances (Jarrett) Thompson, migrated to Worcester, Massachusetts in 1938, the year of the great hurricane. I can remember some of her accounts of that storm. If the reader is to understand my mother's position in the Jarrett family, there are a few things that she/he should know. The first important fact is that my great grandparents, who were mentioned previously, had nine children: four girls and five boys. All of their girls were either still born or died shortly after birth. When their son, Robert Lee, married and his first child was born, also a boy, the family began to wonder if there would ever be a girl for them. So you can imagine their joy when their son Hugh's wife gave birth to a health, beautiful baby girl. From the day of her birth, the entire family adored her. I suppose one could say that she was spoiled. However, spoiled for poor working people is never as comfortable as it is for the affluent. Mother knew and appreciated the survival struggle. And, of course, she worked as long as her health permitted.

They tell me that I was less than two years old when my father died in a farm accident. It was he who named me. Unfortunately, I remember nothing about Joseph Thompson. The image that I have of him is based on what my mother and other family members have told me. I have often wondered what events in my life would have been different, if he had lived.

The sudden death of her husband made it necessary for mother to find work that paid enough to support her and her child. She had limited formal education, having quit school to marry when she was fifteen years old. This was much against her father's will. My grandfather held my father totally responsible for her decision, and never forgave him. He refused to accept that fact that his daughter was the strong willed one. Even though she was a minor, he (grandfather) gave in to her wishes and permitted her to enter this marriage that she thought she wanted. In any event, widowed at seventeen with an infant on her hands, she decided to become part of the northern migration and join her father and uncle in Massachusetts. Of course, the only practical thing to do was leave her infant daughter on the farm with Momma and

Granddaddy. Being a skilled and creative seamstress, she left Tennessee in 1938 with the promise of a new life "up north."

She never discussed her hopes, dreams or experiences with me. As it turned out, our time together was brief and perhaps she though that I was too young to understand. That may have been so. But, I was not too young to remember so many things about her. Her very delicate physical appearance, her beauty, gentleness and uncanny talent for creativity, as well as an instant temper, limited her patience, but never her love.

I suspect that mother met the second Joseph in her life on the day in 1938 that she stepped off the train at Union Station in Worcester, Massachusetts. Joseph Perkins was his name, and I also suspect that Joseph Perkins probably decided that he was going to marry her, the first time he saw her. The length of their courtship was extended by caution on my mother's part and perhaps a need to *experience* a bit of the fun that young people need to experience before taking on marital responsibilities.

Things seemed to go well for mother. She eventually married Joe and they moved into the first floor apartment of his mother's three-decker at 31 Laurel Street. This second marriage made it possible for mother to make plans to have me with her again.

In spite of my father's death and the need for my mother to leave me at such an early age, my "imprint" years were marvelous. From my first moment of awareness I thought that my great grandparents were my mother and father, and as I mentioned previously, Ben was my brother. These were the roles that they played, and they played them well.

Now, my mother had returned to take me from the only world that I had ever known. Next year (1939) after my sixth birthday, I would also migrate to the north. It would be fun to ride the train for the first time. But I hated to leave Momma and Granddaddy and I would surely miss Ben, my hero and my friend. I would see him only twice more before his death, and within three years my beautiful mother would also die, would never see our farm again. Two years after I left, Granddaddy was forced to sell his land to the Government and move his family to a place called the Summit.

CHAPTER. II

The Complexity of Causes

HISTORY IS RECORDED in accordance with the perception and the prospectus of its recorders. Regardless of how objective one tries to be, one cannot deny this frailty of humanness. That is why it is so imperative for those who find themselves categorized as "minorities" in a society to be the recorders of their own history. And make every effort to assure that nothing is lost. The significance of events sometimes is not fully realized until long after the events have passed.

> The accounts of the last quarter of the nineteenth century and entry into the twentieth have been written with the blood of Negroes. In the last sixteen years of the nineteenth century, there had been more than 2,500 lynchings—Mississippi, Alabama, Georgia and Louisiana leading the nation. In the very first year of the new century, more than 100 Negroes were lynched and, before the outbreak of World War I, the number for the century had soared to more than 1,100.[1]

1 J.H. Franklin, From Slavery To Freedom, New York: Vintage Books, 1969, P.439, 453.

President Wilson promised, "I want to assure them (Negroes) that should I become President of the United States they may count upon me for absolute fair dealing, for everything by which I could assist in advancing the interest of their race in the United States."[2] Wilson's administration received the greatest flood of bills proposing discriminatory legislation against Negroes that had ever been introduced into an American Congress: Segregation in public carriers in the District of Columbia, exclusion from commissions in the Army and Navy, separate accommodations for black and white federal employees, and the exclusion of all immigrants of Negro descent. Although most of the legislation failed to pass, Wilson, by executive order, segregated most of the Negro federal employees so far as eating and rest room facilities were concerned. Monroe Trotter, one of the founders and publishers of The Guardian, a Black newspaper dedicated to full and immediate equality for Negroes, protested the segregation of Negro federal employees, but was dismissed from the White House because Wilson regarded his language as insulting.

In 1914, President Wilson issued a proclamation of neutrality. In 1915, he ordered the occupation of Haiti by the Marines in violation of that country's sovereignty and territorial integrity. Hundreds of Haitians were killed to restore peace and order. During this same year, one of Thomas Dixon's violent anti-Negro writings had been made into a motion picture titled "The Birth of a Nation". Its release increased the lynchings and other forms of violence across the Nation. Northern states and the Midwest were not excluded, although the numbers of their killings were nowhere near those of the South.

2 J.H. Franklin, From Slavery To Freedom, New York: Vintage Books, 1969, P.439, 453.

It was an extensively distressful year. Booker T. Washington's death left Negroes without a known and respected leader. His death resulted in the forming of an American Conference of Distinguished Negroes who drew up resolutions to work quietly and earnestly for the enfranchisement of the Negro, the abolition of lynching, and the enforcement of the laws protecting civil liberties. These black leaders of the United States sought relentlessly to acquire in their country the democracy that the allies were seeking to extend to the entire world.

When the insanity of war spread its shroud over the earth in 1914, Americans were not prepared to be a part of the madness. Preoccupied with their own domestic problems and Woodrow Wilson's promise of a "New Freedom", their attention was focused on the economic and social maladjustments that resulted from the previous generation's great industrial upheaval.[3] This statement was even more so for Negroes who had no ties or interest in Europe and even, more importantly, had overwhelming demands made on their attention and energy just trying to survive in America.

Reconstruction had left a bitter taste. They were skeptical of the Democratic Party and did not necessarily feel any trust toward the first President of southern origin to occupy the White House since the Civil War. Their political situation, to say the least, had gone from bad to worse.[4] Roosevelt's determination of guilty without a trial and dishonorable dismissal of the entire Twenty-Fifth regiment, disqualifying its members for service in either the military or the civil service, added to the Negroes' skepticism. The Twenty-Fifth was a Negro

3 J.H. Franklin, From Slavery To Freedom, New York: Vintage Books 1969, P.452, 453, 442.

4 J.H. Franklin, From Slavery To Freedom, New York: Vintage Books 1969, P.452, 453, 442.

battalion stationed at Fort Brown.[5] Three companies of the battalion had become involved in a race riot in Brownsville, Texas. With very limited options available, Negroes decided that Roosevelt, in spite of this, was better than Taft, and they hoped that Roosevelt would assure them that the new party would stand unequivocally for full citizenship for the Negro.

When the war came in 1914, Hugh, my grandfather, was too young to go. "Thank God!" "It doesn't make sense for our boys to go, to die in some God forsaken place over the seas." William E. B. DuBois had been wrong when he encouraged black men to join the military. His theory was that full citizenship and human respect would be granted to Afro Americans if they fought for "their country". Those were Momma's thoughts, expressed through two World Wars. She knew that in spite of everything, Hugh, her eldest son, wanted to go. What is it about some males that make them hunger to be warriors? Some will participate in any man's war to satisfy this need. Hugh talked frequently about the Ninth and Tenth Cavalries and the Twenty-Fourth Infantries. These were the Negro units of the Regular Army. There were 10,000 black men in these units and another 10,000 in various units of the National Guard. Ironically, Hugh never became a warrior; he was too young for the First War and too old for the Second. Instead, he donated a son, his eldest.

One of the most important social and economic phenomena on the home front was the migration of hundreds of Negroes out of the South during the War. The fundamental cause of the exodus was economic, though there were certainly some important social considerations. The severe labor depression in the South in 1914 and 1915 sent wages down

---

5 J.H. Franklin, From Slavery To Freedom, New York: Vintage Books 1969, P.452, 453, 442.

to 75 cents per day and less....the boll weevil and floods destroyed crops and left many southerners destitute and homeless...while the wheels of Northern industry were turning more rapidly than ever, and the demand for laborers was increasing.... foreign immigration had declined from more than one million in 1914 to slightly more than three hundred thousand in 1915. There was a labor shortage. The Negro press persuaded Southern Negroes to abandon the existence, which held nothing better than second-class citizenship. The Chicago Defender exclaimed, "To die from frost is far more glorious than at the hands of a mob". The Pennsylvania Railroad brought 12,000 to work in its yards and on its tracks. My grandfather worked for years for the Providence and Worcester Railroad, at the Worcester Round House. He was a fireman. It was estimated that by the end of 1918, more than one million Negroes had left the South. White southerners became alarmed. Jacksonville, Florida passed an ordinance requiring migration agents to pay a license fee of $1,000. White citizens of many Southern towns threatened Negroes. Homes were without servants; farms were without laborers.

It was a complex set of circumstances that launched my family into the northern migration. A marriage that failed and ultimately ended in divorce contributed to Ben's father, Robert Lee's decision to go. He was the third son, and the most adventurous. I have not been able to determine why he chose to settle in Massachusetts, particularly the city of Worcester.

People married very young in those days, and Hugh, the oldest son, and my grandfather was no exception. However, after only five years of marriage, my grandmother died. He remained in Tennessee for a few years, finding work where and when he could to support himself and his daughter. Finally, he decided that it would be better to go north and get a "good paying job" that would allow him to send money back home for my mother's support, and a little to help his mother and father. Hearing that the best wages were paid by the Steel Mills, he went to Pennsylvania. For a while at least, good fortune was with him. He landed a job and worked the steel mills until the economy slowed down and he was laid off.

Uncle Robert Lee was the kind of man who mastered situations rather than allowing situations to master him. He managed somehow to acquire a franchise and open his own filling station in Worcester. It was his encouragement that persuaded my grandfather to leave Pennsylvania and come to Massachusetts to help him run his filling station. This worked out nicely for grandfather, and provided some immediate income while he was still trying to get settled. At that time, he could continue sending money home whenever he could to pay for my mother's support. It was during his first year in Worcester that he met Lillian, the woman who was to become his second wife, and bear him two sons, Robert and Arthur. Lillian, or Lill, as everyone called her, was a large woman, who was very fair and plain, but not totally unattractive. Evidently, she was a sensuous woman who had a tendency to overindulge. She was a compulsive eater but that wasn't the worst of her activities. She also had a weakness for other men. In fact, after several years of marriage, she eventually left grandfather for another man, one much younger than herself. That was a blow to my grandfather's ego from which he would never completely recover. It's a strange phenomenon. In spite of the fact that Momma and Granddaddy were married well over 50 years, each of their sons was married at least twice. And all but one had been divorced, except Williard. His first wife died of cancer.

The Jarrett men always had a lot of fun when they got

together. They used to sit laughing and talking for hours. I remember once when Uncle Williard was in Worcester on a visit, I heard them talking about their wives. Uncle Williard said something to the effect that if a man wants to make sure that he will keep a wife and have a minimum of domestic problems, he should marry the ugliest woman that he can find. She will never leave for anyone else because no other man would want her. And she'll be so grateful to her husband for marrying her in the first place, that she will be the perfect, obedient wife. They shared belly laughs on this one. But, the whole family knew that my grandfather had tried to do just that when choosing his third wife. They *were* married on Christmas day 1937. By far, Hannahbell Bennerman, wife number three, was the most physically unattractive woman that I have ever seen. Short and round would have described her best in those days. Her most prominent facial feature was a nose that seemed to take up most of her face and left little room for eyes that were too small and lips that were too full.

Her extremely dark face was usually set in a scowl and that was framed by very sparse hair. She wore the scowl for a reason. Because, in addition to everything else that I have mentioned, Hannahbell was, and still is, the personification of evil. But all humans have their vanity, in spite of the odds. As strange as it may seem, this woman's source of pride were her feet. In spite of her weight, her bones were small, and she had very small feet with very high arches. And she frequently made comments about her beautiful feet and legs. She wore only Van Raalte hosiery that she used to buy at Barnards' department store and only the best in shoes.

To say that my grandfather was a hard working man, is putting it mildly. One need only look at his accomplishments to appreciate the extent of his ambition. Like all of his brothers, with the exception of Uncle Ted, he could read, write and had a natural ability to cipher.

None of them had high school diplomas. Grandfather's first land purchase in Massachusetts was a small cottage off route 70 in Shrewsbury. A few years after moving to Shrewsbury, he purchased a one hundred and fifty acre farm in Upton. He planned on eventually turning the farm over to his oldest son, Bob, but fate willed that that would never happen. To reach this level of prosperity, grandfather worked a full eleven to seven shift at the round house. He also purchased a truck and started a rubbish and garbage collection business. There were many times, while his sons were away in the military, that he would come home, put his lunch bucket down, change his clothes and take the truck out to do the day's route. He was a man who loved the land and seemed most at home while working with the soil or with animals. He made his garbage collection business pay off by developing a hog farm. In addition to hogs, he also kept chickens and usually eight or nine cows. I have mentioned all of this so that the reader can understand how a man can live day to day and year to year without ever knowing or sensing the forces that are at work in his own house.

Small Brown Goose

THE CHILDREN OF the Jarrett family have always been the nomenclatures for each generation. This caused some confusion for outsiders. For example, Momma was called Momma by her children, grandchildren and first generation great grandchildren. It was the fourth and fifth generation of children who decided to call her Little Momma. Uncle Ted was called Uncle Ted by all of us, even his own daughters, who still refer to him as uncle. Whatever name of affection the children chose, seemed to last a lifetime. This was extremely confusing to outsiders. In order to clarify things in this writing, I decided to call my mother, Mother, which I never did in fact. And, my grandfather, whom I always—called Dad, I refer to here as grandfather.

In early spring 1939, granddaddy and my mother carried me and two suitcases to the back of the bus. I can't recollect their conversation during that ride to town. I was so bewildered; this was a bittersweet experience. Anxiety over leaving Momma, Granddaddy and Ben, the fear of leaving the familiarity of the farm, coupled with forlornness as though we would never *see* each other again. On the other hand, I was excited to be taking my first train ride. I'd heard the adults talk about "up north;" now I was going there to live. I rode into Chattanooga with all of these emotions churning inside me.

Granddaddy checked our suitcases and we walked around to the loading platform, climbed into the colored only car and found seats. Before long the conductor sang out "Bo-a-r'd, all a board." Granddaddy kissed us good-bye and then left the car and stood on the platform. The big engine chocked and puffed, struggling to move its burden, as the conductor continued to call out to latecomers. The wheels caught and we moved painfully forward. A very little girl with large sad eyes pressed her nose against the window and looked at a man who was waving and saying good-bye with a smile while his *eyes* brimmed with tears. The child's eyes remained large and sad, and for her the tears would not come. He grew smaller as the train pulled away from the platform, a sad lonely figure. As I watched there was a sudden confrontation of all of the emotions that had been churning around inside of me. I felt a kind of inner hysteria and coldness; the tears came.

It wasn't long before I put sadness aside. It is truly wonderful to be just on this side of infancy and taking your first train ride. I had never seen much more than our farm, so you can imagine the effect that this had on me. I wished the train would slow down and let me see more; my imagination went wild.

We had a three-hour layover in New York, which gave us time for some sightseeing. There are things that I will never forget: Grand Central Station with its ceiling of twinkling stars, the Empire State Building (that was the world's tallest in those days) and all of the people. I had never seen so many people. I was still churning with excitement when we boarded a train in Grand Central for the last lap of our journey. Before long the conductor could be heard announcing the next stop in the special voice one octave below music:

"W-o-oster, next stop W-o-o-ster".

In a few minutes our train pulled into the Union Station, we are home...(you can never go back).

There's something special about the Union Station. Even now, neglected and abused, it retains its beauty and arrogance. I stepped out on its platform while the station was in its prime. And I have spent hours playing on its marble stairs. I imagine one could still hear the echo of voices if one were to go inside, stand very still and listen.

My stepfather was a red cap; this was considered to be a very good job-out of the few that were open to blacks. He carried suitcases for tips, a discount on train tickets and I suppose for the minimum wage. To make it more interesting, he had to outrun several other red caps to get what they called "good tips". Nevertheless, this did not affect my love for the station or the joy that I felt watching the trains come and go.

From the beginning, it was obvious that Joe's life centered around. my mother. He took full advantage of his ticket discount and every weekend that summer (when he didn't have to work) we went somewhere. We saw the New York World's Fair with its sphere and steeple; we shopped in Macy's and Gimble's and took a trip to Nantasket so that I could see the ocean for the first time.

So Joe did all that he could to delight his bride, while she concentrated on delighting me; we were inseparable. She left me once to find work after my father's death, and now it was almost as though she had vowed that only an act of God would separate us again...perhaps he heard her.

Summer was gone. The early morning and late afternoon coolness that seems to purge the air before frost, had forced us into sweaters. It was time for me to register for school. With only a one-room country school in my past, Elizabeth Street School impressed me like it has never impressed anyone else. I couldn't wait for classes to start. But it wasn't going to be quite that easy because when this strange looking kid with the oversized eyes and that weird way of talking (that Tennessee accent almost destroyed me), entered that building, she immediately became "the runt of the litter". I became everyone's target, black and white.

If I could have kept my mouth shut, things might not have been so bad. But, that's something that I have never learned to do. Anyway I still loved school. These confrontations always occurred after school, so I began to think of ways to outsmart them. For a couple of days, the minute the bell rang I'd take off down Elizabeth Street over to Laurel Street. Jesse Owens had nothing on me. In addition to being the most beat up kid on the block, I was also the fastest. Well this didn't last long. Soon they began to cut me off at Jakes' store. This went on for a couple of weeks. Then one afternoon just as one little chap was about to clobber me, he stopped short, turned and ran. I looked around and there stood my mother. She didn't say a word to me or anyone else. She just took my hand and we walked home. I felt great because I thought she was going to continue to meet me after school. This was a short-lived joy. When we go home, she sat me down in the kitchen and then she said, "Young lady, I don't want you to every come home crying again because that little boy or some other boy or girl hit you. From now on you make the kids leave you alone." I nearly had heart failure. It wasn't so bad getting hit if everything was fine at home, but now mother was upset, and if I came home crying I just might get a licking.

I barely ate my supper; I just sat there listening to my

heart pound. Thinking, "this may be the last time that I hear it. They're going to kill me tomorrow." That was the shortest night of my life. I walked to school the next morning with all the enthusiasm of a condemned man walking the last mile. I kept to myself all day thinking, "maybe they won't notice me and forget that I'm here. Please God don't let anybody hit me." He wasn't listening, and my legs were too rubbery from fear to run. So, when the bell rang I walked right to my assailant and stood there. Granddaddy used to say that a scared man will kill you quicker than anybody, especially if he's cornered. I was scared and in sheer terror. I closed my eyes and lit into that kid with all the strength and fury that I could muster. He let out one yelp and took off across the street like all the demons of hell were after him. That was my last fight at Elizabeth Street School.

Fall gradually turned to winter, Christmas was almost upon us. We went to the Radio City Christmas show to celebrate. When we came home it snowed with all the delicate loveliness that the first snow brings. I missed Ben, Momma and Granddaddy and that touch of sadness surfaced again.

That Christmas I received my first sled. Nothing could have pleased me more. There was no shortage of snow. It would pile up to the window sill of the first floor of our old three decker and stay there till spring. There were no facilities for snow removal. And the snow would pile up so high on the streets that you couldn't see the people walking on the sidewalk on the other side. Every street had its own igloo and fortress structure, a tribute to young sculptors. The streets were ours; there were very few vehicles. Those that were rolling used chains that made it possible for us to hear them a block away. We would hop on our sleds, push off at the top of Laurel Street, build up full speed midway and cut the corner at Carol Street. Sometimes we'd steer into a snow bank to make it interesting.

Jean's party is the thing that I recall best about that winter. Jean's mother had died a few years before. She and her father had moved in with his mother, Grandma Perkins. That made it possible for Mrs. Perkins to take over the chore of raising the child. Ma Perkins (as everyone called her) hated the New England winters. She said the cold made her bones ache. She must have thought Jean's ached too. Because she used to put so many layers of under shirts and bloomers on her that she always looked chubby in the winter even though she was naturally a long skinny kid. Of course we teased her about her bloomers all winter. Bloomers or not, Jean was the apple of her father's *eye* and her birthday was always a special occasion. I had a new dress and new shoes just for the affair.

My mother had bundled me up and given me strict orders to come home the minute I started feeling cold. Usually I played right on my own street and if my mother wanted me she would just come to the door or window. I don't know why I did it. But, I decided to follow the gang over to Prospect Street and try some new turf. We had a grand time. Before I knew it, it was past noon. I noticed that my feet felt a little numb as I walked home. My mother was furious she had been looking for me and calling for hours, I had stayed out far too long. By the time *she* got my boots, shoes and socks off I was in the middle of a severe case of chilblains, and screaming at the top of my lungs. I could see my feet swelling and I swear they seemed to be on fire. Warm water stopped the pain but the swelling was there to stay for a few days. The last thing that I wanted to do was go to Jean's party; my feet looked like loaves of bread. To make bad matters worse, my mother put heavy woolen socks on me and then pulled my beat up old bedroom slippers over them. I wanted to go somewhere and hide. But, instead, she took my hand and walked me upstairs to the party.

Winter in Tennessee is cold and harsh at times, but blessedly brief, mostly. It's a flirtation that suddenly gives. way to a flood of honeysuckle, dogwood and the pink, white and blue bells of morning glories. New England winters are more serious and after December became so persistent that it seemed, even to me, that it would never end. However, it did, and just as it was relinquishing its power to spring, my mother caught an abominable cold that almost developed into pneumonia.

It took several weeks of rest and medication to get her up and about again. Still, she didn't feel just right and the cough persisted.

It *was* summer with promises of trips to the beach, clam fritters, and all the "good stuff" that goes with summer.

She was delicate by nature, tall, five feet nine, and slim as a willow, only now she began to look drawn and tired. In those days there were three black doctors in the city. Until recently, one of them, Dr. Goldsberry, still lived in the same house that he lived in thirty-eight years ago, on what is now called Goldsberry Street. Out of the three, how or why we wound up with Dr. MacKerrow, I will never understand. Anyway, I have a mental image of him that I will never lose. He was round, not rotund because he was not exceptionally large, just round. There were no sharp edges or corners about him. That's why his waxed mustache with its pointed ends gave him the appearance of a carved doll. The ends of that mustache were so pointed that you would have expected him to skewer anything that came within range. He was known as the pill doctor. In fact people always said that he made his own pills. He had a special room for that purpose in the back of his old house on Elliot Street. If you broke your leg, instead of a cast, MacKerrow gave you pills. Mother was no exception. After examining her, he walked out of her room, reached into that mysterious black bag and came forth with three bottles of pills which he placed on the table, as he gave Joe specific instruction on their proper administration. I must say that if bedside manner could cure illness he would have won a Nobel Prize, because he was over-endowed with that quality. My mother took his pills. When one wants and expects to get better the mind will sometimes fool the body. It was this way with her; she actually seemed to improve.

In fact, she felt so much better that she and my grandfather planned a special surprise for my birthday. I knew he was coming to see me so when I heard his truck in the driveway I ran to the door. When he opened the door he held a large cardboard box under his left arm. He stood smiling for a moment. Then he held the box in front of him, said "Happy Birthday Sweetheart" and bent over to let me *see* the surprise. Looking up from the box were two brown eyes, a button nose, and two floppy ears attached to what I thought was the most wonderful puppy that I had ever seen. Grandpa said he was part German Shepard and the rest was just dog but to me he was wonderful. It was instant love. For some crazy reason, probably lack of imagination, I named him Buster.

I never really liked dolls because they aren't real. They just sit there and stare no matter what happens. A puppy never sits any place for more than half a minute. The living room, dining room and bedrooms were out of bounds, but the rest of the house was ours. When we weren't playing in the yard or taking walks, we were running through our part of the house. About three weeks after Buster joined our family, my mother was taking her evening medication and accidentally dropped one of her pills. Before anyone could grab him, Buster lapped it up and twenty minutes later he died.

Farm children live with birth and death; they are part of the farm routine. I had seen and touched dead animals. Granddaddy slaughtered our meat and occasionally a cow or hog would die of natural causes. But this was the first time that death had taken something that I loved. There were no questions before. This was my first real encounter with death. My mother tried to comfort me and while I was still sobbing, Ma Perkins came downstairs. She hugged me and asked if the puppy had made me happy. This was such a strange question that I stopped crying and just sat there in my mother's lap and looked at her. Then she said, "Your puppy's job was done. None of us are here to stay. We are just visitors; some have shorter visits than others." Years later, I would remember that statement.

The extent of pain cannot be accurately measured or determined by one viewing the event. Instead, the individuals' mental and physical tolerance for pain must be considered together with the intensity of the event. After Buster's death, sadness never left us. My mother grew worse, and by the time school started, she was confined to bed. One day, when I cam home from school, I went to her room and found her clutching the side of the bed with tears streaming down her cheeks. The pain was so intense that she could hardly speak. This was the only time that I ever saw my mother cry. I didn't know what to do. She had always been the comforter; she made my pains go away, but there was nothing that I could do for her. Grandpa had been trying to get her to *see* another doctor and the next day she did. Thursday morning I got up and dressed while Joe fixed my breakfast. I went in, kissed my mother good-bye and went to school as usual. That was the last time that I touched her or heard her voice. While I was in school, Joe took her to the hospital.

The sadness came closer and closer to the surface and the band around my heart grew tighter. I found myself capsulated in a segment of time that was long because of loneliness. And, at the same time short because I sensed the determining factor at its end.

Children under twelve years of age were not allowed in hospitals. So, I wrote her letters that Joe delivered every day. I saw her twice more. Once on my birthday, to let her *see* how I had grown and again in the fall. She sent me a reply on my birthday, written on powder blue stationery. I still have that letter pressed between the pages of my Bible.

> Darling,
>
> I am so sorry I am late in sending you a birthday present. Thanks so much for the nice letter. You are writing much better. Here is a dollar for your piggy bank. All my love.
>
> Your Mother

By fall she had grown so weak that she could no longer leave her bed. I had to stand some distance away on the side of the hill in order to see the second floor window. I could only *see* a small figure looking down and waving. She waved for a minute, then stopped, and just looked down at me until the nurse pushed her bed back to the center of the room.

> Frances J. Perkins, 26, of 31 Laurel St. died last night after a long illness. She leaves a daughter....

Time gives no consideration to pain. It pushes us along and takes its toll without consent or concern for our readiness.

I went back to Tennessee for a while and it was good. A "Balm in Gilead", that helped me through the years that would follow when I returned to my grandfather's house in New England. I always called my grandfather Dad, because that's what my mother called him. Anyway, when I went to live with him, he was married to Hannahbell, his third wife. Hannahbell truly hated my mother; perhaps because Dad and the rest of the family loved her so. Whatever her reasons were, she turned that hate to *me,* I believed, because I was Frances' daughter and I was vulnerable. I went to live with them about two years before the country entered World War II.

My grandfather was such a gentle soul. I never could understand why he married Hannahbell. She never let him or Uncle Bob know how cruel she was, and I never told them. Dad had enough on his mind as I mentioned previously. He worked nights for the railroad, had his own trucking business and the farm. Uncle Bob did most of the trucking and farming until he was drafted then the whole burden *was* on Dad and the few 4F's and/or alcoholics in town that he could get to work a few days a week.

He used to come in from his night job, eat, change clothes and take the truck out to pick up rubbish. When he finally got home in the afternoon, he'd eat again and sleep a few hours before leaving for the round house. I only saw him on Sundays.

It didn't take me long to realize that Hannahbell's cruelty towards me was more than jealousy. She *was* actually trying to destroy me physically and mentally. She saw me as a threat to her security. Her fears increased after Bob's death. He was to be her heir. He was the only member of the Jarrett family that she approved of. I must explain that Hannahbell was not stupid. She was poorly educated, as were most blacks who migrated from the south. Like her brethren, she was ignorant about *many* things due to a lack of experience. However, Hannahbell was a very clever, very devious woman. Finding herself without an heir, and never being able to conceive a child, she decided to adopt one of her cousin's children. Her scheme fell through when she discovered that she and Dad were too old to adopt a child in the state of Massachusetts. They did take the infant in and raised her as their own.

Meanwhile, Hannahbell was left with the task of getting rid of me. How hard she tried. It was an impossible task. I had inherited my mother's determination and fighting spirit. Also, I must have inherited a bit of extra stamina from my father. I have to admit that I did not come out of that experience unscathed. In fact, it cost me two years of my life. Two years spent in a hospital while my body struggled to mend. Memories of Momma, Granddaddy, Ben and the farm in Tennessee, linked with memories of my mother and all of the affection that I had known kept me mentally strong. This was important because I was too young to understand that Hannahbell was lashing out in fear. Her abuse was very diverse; she was a creative woman. Her favorite activity of course, were beatings. Once, she stripped me and forced me to kneel in front of a chair in the kitchen to take my punishment. I have scars that I will carry to my grave from that one. When she couldn't think of anything else to do, she would make a fist and grind her knuckles into my skull. Usually she did this when she had to walk by, just to let me know she was in charge. My chores consisted of cleaning the barn and hog pens, feeding the animals, scrubbing the floors, washing and waxing woodwork, shampooing rugs, washing windows and anything else she could think of. There were few nights that I managed to get to bed before eleven or twelve. My mental torment was worse. I adored my mother; she was as wonderful and good in my sight as Hannahbell was evil. Having been raised as a Southern Baptist, my mother lived by the Baptist moral code.

For example, she never wore makeup because she considered it indecent, nor did she drink, swear or smoke. In this day and age such a statement sounds ridiculous, but that is the way it used to be. I only mention this because Hannahbell aimed her verbal attacks at my mother, knowing that any cruelty against my mother would be far more painful to me than anything that she could do to me personally. She loved to say to me, "your mother was a diseased dog and a whore." Any response in defense of my mother was an excuse for a beating, because I was being disrespectful in talking back. It took a while before I became smart enough to control my emotions; she could only see the pain in my eyes.

Uncle Bob left for boot camp, I missed him. During that first year in my grandfather's house, he had become my only friend. I was not allowed to have other friends. He taught me to love music, to play chess and helped me to laugh for the joy of laughing. For a while he erased the sadness but now he was in the Philippines and Dad's baby brother Williard was in Burma. I was still too young to appreciate the seriousness of a war being fought so far away. We bought bonds, collected cans and struggled like everyone with rationing. Finally, it was over and the armed forces were coming home.

Bob had only been gone a year but I recall wondering why he looked so old and tired. That was a happy day for us, even Lady, Dad's old German Shepard, was happy. Lady had also become my friend. We used to play in Demarios' apple orchard whenever I could get a break. She insisted on following me everywhere that I went. When I left for school in the morning, Hannahbell had to keep her in the house until the bus left. So, I had Lady and Uncle Bob had come back from the war without a scratch. I was happy.

He never talked much about the war. Realizing that he didn't want to talk about it, I never asked questions. He bought me a necklace made of shells while he was over there. I still have it. He did tell us once about having to dig foxholes with his bare hands when the enemy airplanes came. That was behind him now. Like the rest of the country, we busied ourselves with living. We thanked God that there was no small banner of stars in our window.

About three months later, after Dad left for work, we had all gone to bed. I had to be sleeping soundly because I did not hear a sound, only Hannahbell heard Uncle Bob cry out. I can only repeat her words, "When I went in he was having a fit, his eyes were rolled back into his head and he was foaming at the mouth." Once again I felt the sadness.

It was grand mal epilepsy caused by snail fever. The doctors determined that Bob had contracted the germ through the pores of his skin from the soil in the Philippines. He didn't stay in the hospital long. Dad and Hannahbell were given instructions on what to do to keep him from biting his tongue or choking on it when he had a seizure. He returned to the hospital periodically for tests. He hadn't told us the whole story. The doctors couldn't locate the germ, only the antibody and if they didn't find it soon....

Hannahbell called me in to go to the store for her. She gave me specific instructions not to take Lady. This was a problem, because I couldn't catch her to put her in the house. Every time I told her to go home, she would turn around as though she was going and hide until I started to walk again.

By the time I got to the road I thought she had given up and gone home. I stood across from the rows of mailboxes on Route 70, waited for a car to pass, then crossed as a trailer truck appeared around the corner. I continued toward the store until I heard the screech of brakes. Then I turned. The truck had run over Lady's hindquarters. With her last ounce of strength, she struggled to pull herself up, then collapsed and died.

Uncle Bob grew weary of the needles and examinations; he also began to lose his memory. He continued to work on the farm and he never lost hope. We rarely played chess now. He still found comfort in his music and he would sit for hours in the evening playing records as he did that night until almost midnight. Dad got up to go to work and the rest of us went to bed. The next morning, when my uncle didn't come down to breakfast as usual, I went upstairs to wake him. He had had his final seizure.

> Robert L. Jarrett, 26, died last night at home, 21 Eaton Avenue, Shrewsbury. He leaves a niece

Life happens to us in measured segments that are filled with events to bring us to turning points. Motivation, emotion, and intellect explain why individuals make the choices that they do. For some, the more turbulent and painful the events, the more profound the turning point. Through it all, we are manipulated by some force that puts obstacles in our path, that causes events, that predetermines our major decisions without relieving us of responsibility.

CHAPTER IV

Well-Nigh A Woman

WE HAD FREEZING rain last night, the kind that turns suburban streets into glass caverns and covers trees with ice crystal lace. Transparent stalactites sway gently, then small branches sound like crystalline wind chimes as their fragile covers fall and shatter sending tiny sparkles flying across my hood and windshield.

It was 1948, when I drove Dad's old pickup truck into Worcester to look for my first job. I didn't want to quit school and I certainly wasn't looking forward to the fact that I would eventually have to move into town and live alone. My courage had not caught up to my needs.

This situation was compounded by the fact that there were few job options available to Blacks in Worcester. The level of one's education didn't matter; it was the color of one's skin that was important. Black male college graduates were employed as chauffeurs and porters. Women had a choice between cleaning, either as a domestic or in a public building, running elevators in stores or office buildings, or filling an unskilled position in a shop. The lucky women got jobs in shops. Shops paid more than stores and anything paid more than domestic work. The very lucky women managed to get into shops that trained them to stich. They got piecework and made a good week's pay. When times were good and the orders were coming in, some of them could make from one hundred to two hundred dollars in one week. They had to be careful not to do that too often, because the rate setter would cut the rate. I used to dream about making one hundred dollars a week.

Filling out job applications was a painful process. One of the questions always asked was the date of the applicant's graduation from high school. It was humiliating to admit that I had not completed high school. Those experiences reinforced my determination to go back to school and get my diploma. I don't remember the names of the places that the Unemployment Office sent me to. However, I discovered that I could get a job, be it ever so humble. To this day, I have never collected unemployment compensation.

My first paying job was working as a buck press operator at Barry Sports Wear. It was a cheap little sweatshop on the second floor of the Stevens Walden Building on Shrewsbury Street. The shop was owned by a man named Feldman. He was a small, balding man, probably in his late fifties, and he wore rather thick glasses. His shop produced women's three-piece suits in a synthetic linen that was red, green and brown. Stevens Walden made tools, wrenches I believe, and they were known to be one of the dirtiest shops in the city. Upstairs wasn't much better; the only thing missing was the grease. In addition, it was hot and the cheap synthetic fabric and dye released such a foul odor when the steam hit it that for a while it made me sick. But I adjusted, and before long putting in eight hours a day was a piece of cake. After all, I had been accustomed to much longer hours and much harder work for much less compensation.

Feldman was a demanding taskmaster who failed to deal fairly with his employees. If there was the slightest defect in a suit, we heard about it. The shop was located on the edge of the Italian neighborhood, not far from the Black East Side. Close to cheap labor.

One man worked in the shop as a cutter. He would come in once a week or as needed and cut bolts to fill orders. The rest of the staff members were women, mostly Italian, immigrants and Blacks. He hired the Italians for less than he would have had to pay Americans and he hired the Blacks for less than he paid the Italians. It was supposed to be a union shop. The steward came in periodically. If the Italians complained, Feldman would give them a penny or so more on their rates after talking to the steward. They never did anything for the Blacks. Black women were never allowed to stich in that shop. We all paid union dues but the union only spoke for a few and it wasn't even honest in its dealings with them.

I became such a thorn in Feldman's side that he promised me a raise just to shut me up. Unfortunately, he died before I could collect. Barry Sports Wear was a story in itself. I won't use the names of the people because I'm sure that some of them are still around. Laura was an American of Italian descent; she and I were the only buck press operators. We pressed the large flat sections of the garments and the women on the steam irons did the touch up work, i.e. seams and shoulders. I never have figured out where he sold those suits—they were by far the ugliest, cheapest looking garments that I had ever seen. Anyway, Laura was the daughter-in-law of Clara, an Italian immigrant, who was the senior stitcher or, I should say, employee. Clara wielded the unstructured power in the shop, she was the oldest and a matriarch kind of figure. The rumor was that Clara carried a knife in her stocking.

I never saw it or gave it a lot of thought. I liked Clara. But there was a strange arrangement between Laura, Feldman and Clara.

Another rumor was that Laura was a kind of mistress to Feldman. A couple of times each week they would go to his office at the back of the shop for twenty minutes or so. Laura and I talked quite a bit but she never told me what went on in the boss' office. Whatever it was, he literally drooled over Laura and whenever she wanted a raise for herself or Clara, or just for fun, she would stop talking to him. This meant that Feldman spent most of that day at her machine pleading for forgiveness. Most of the time he didn't even know what for. They were a comical couple. She was a little taller than I am, approximately five feet nine. She had the flattest behind that I have ever seen; it simply did not seem to exist. But what she lacked on the bottom she made up for on the top, because on that end she was built like Dolly Parton. To emphasize her assets, she always wore straight skirts with sweaters or very tight knit tops. Poor Mr. Feldman. I felt sorry for him at times. One of the most irritating habits that he had was to call everybody deary. Probably, Laura and Clara were the only ones that he knew by name. In spite of the frustration, we laughed a lot in that shop. The people were warm and friendly and someone was always playing a joke on someone else, especially when Feldman wasn't on the floor. We had a signal, one of the few Italian words that I learned. Whoever saw the boss entering the shop sounded the alarm in Italian. It sounded like "movan-movan": They told us non-Italians that it meant he comes; I hope so.

Christmas at Barrys was one big Italian party. There were trays of pasta, pastry, liquor and wine. I tasted stuffed squid for the first time at Barry Sports Wear.

After working for several months, I bought my first automobile. There was no bus service between Upton and Worcester. The only way for me to get to work was to ride in on the truck. On days when both trucks were not being used, I would drive one to work. I learned to drive when I was fifteen. I started driving the tractor and the trucks around the farm. By the time I was sixteen I could drive as well as any of the hands. Better than some. When Dad had his first coronary, I acquired more road experience, because I had to drive the trucks on the rubbish and garbage route. In spite of my experience, Dad had to co-sign for me to get a registration. A person had to be twenty-one to register a vehicle in Massachusetts.

My first car had to be seen to be appreciated. It was a nineteen thirty-six Ford, four-door sedan. It was black with protruding chrome bumpers that curled inward at both ends. It also had running boards and a simulated sunroof. At least it appeared to be a sunroof. The center of the roof was canvas that had shrunk and cracked in the extremes of the New England weather. When it rained, my back seat passengers had to sit under an umbrella to keep from getting soaked to the skin. Hood ornaments used to be large chrome works of art. The one on my Ford was no exception. It was a Big Mack bulldog, welded on by the previous owner no doubt. People must have laughed when they saw me coming. But to me that little car was elegant. Not only did it provide badly needed transportation to and from work, it also provided more social freedom. I began to meet people and make friends.

Nineteen fifty was the year that Granddaddy had to face the fact that he and Momma could no longer survive off the land in Tennessee. So the decision was made and the last of our family who would migrate left the land and joined the urban crowds—Granddaddy, Momma, Uncle Ted and his two daughters. Uncle Frank was married to a woman from Chattanooga. They built their home in Chattanooga and chose to remain there.

Granddaddy and the family moved into an apartment on Washington Street. After getting settled, both Granddaddy and Uncle Ted found work as custodians at the Wyman Gordon Company. These were the only jobs that they ever had in Worcester. Both of them remained employed by Wyman Gordon until their retirements. Granddaddy's was only five or six years after his employment. He was pushing eighty then, but no one knew it.

Until now, I hadn't realized that I had worked for Barry Sports Wear so long. There was a period of discovery or re-discovery for me during my time there. It was also time to catch up on being young. A lack of normal adolescent experiences and relationships had left me very immature in the way I dealt with people and perceived the world.

Compared to other cities of comparable size, Worcester's black population has always been small. In the 40's and 50's it held at about 1,500. When I was a girl most of the Afro-Americans in the Worcester area recognized one another as residents and members of particular families. So if you met someone in the street, they automatically spoke. This was also an extension of a southern custom. The men used to either tip their hats or touch the brim when speaking to a lady. That was a European custom that I liked. Mr. Webbie Schuler used to give that one a special touch of class.

The majority of Worcester's black citizens lived in two locations, the "East Side" and the "West Side". The East Side encompassed the area from Bell Pond to Lincoln Square east from Belmont Street to the jail on Summer Street. The West Side, I believe, started with Bellevue Street, crossed Chandler to Bluff Street, then west across Park Avenue to Beaver Brook. That is where the Negro baseball team played Providence and/or Boston on Sunday afternoons. The west side was a bit more difficult to define because it was where the more prominent "four hundreds" families lived and there were more white folks living in those neighborhoods also. Blacks were confined to these neighborhoods because white landlords would not rent or sell to them in other urban areas. Rural land sold to blacks was very remote with few conveniences. An example of this was Dad's farm in Upton. It was located across from an old C.C. Camp and the only modern convenience that it had was electricity. It had no running water, no city sewerage system and no close neighbors.

When he purchased the land, there was an old cellar hole, and a dilapidated old barn attached to what appeared to be the farm hands' quarters. The entire structure was in a state of decay. There is a story that the folks in the towns of Upton and Westboro used to tell about the farm. According to the story, it was once a beautiful farm with riding stables. The very wealthy owner chose the spot for its remoteness and beauty. He must have been an eccentric individual, because he also liked to keep his money on the premises instead of in a bank. It seems that one night something happened in that farmhouse that caused the master of the house to murder his wife and set the place on fire. Of course, everything burned to the ground because there was no water available to fight the fire. The money was never found. Because of that story, the locals used to come and dig in the cellar hole and around the barn. But no one ever stayed around until dark. Dad finally had to post the land before building on it and moving in.

Worcester's black community retained its "southern village" atmosphere until the mid 1950's. It began to change when migrant farm workers, who came in to pick apples and other crops, began to stay on after the harvest. Like those before them, the new migrants would settle in for a while and then send for other family members. Another phenomenon that has affected our numbers is The Black Revolution of the sixties. Many new jobs and professions opened up to Afro Americans. Our young people no longer had to leave Worcester to use their college educations. Even when the migration shifted into reverse and became the exodus to the South, Worcester lost very few Black families.

Recorders of Worcester's history usually donate about one and three quarters pages to the subject of "The Negroes". Other ethnic groups receive more space just listing their lineage. Some of them read somewhat like the Book of Genesis in the Old Testament. What is mentioned is the African School for Negro Children and the city's three oldest Negro churches, the oldest of the three being John Street Baptist Church, formerly Mt. Olivet. The other two are St. Andrew's Methodist Church, formerly The African Methodist Episcopal Bethel Church and the African Methodist Zion Church. In most of the recorded history of the city of Worcester, the only Negroes mentioned by name are the ministers of these churches. One of them, Marvin Gibson, baptized me when I was twelve years old. At twelve, I was just as large as I am now, and when Reverend Gibson baptized me, this proved to be a problem, because when he dunked me under, backwards, my feet slipped out from under me and I began to thrash around to get my footing. When I did that, the good Reverend slipped. I was sure we both were going to drown.

When I first came to Worcester, I attended the AME Zion Church. My mother's husband *was* a member there and it was very close to where we lived. For those reasons, my mother became Methodist. The rest of the family remained Southern Baptist until the end. When Christianity was first Africanized, the first formal Negro church in America was The African American Episcopal Church. However, I believe that the Baptist Church has retained more of the atmosphere of the old church, especially in the rural south. Until recently, the church was the nucleus of the Black family's social life.

The only other Negro mentioned in Worcester's history is Willie, a mulatto. Mulatto is kind of hung on to his name as if that fact makes him worth mentioning or, at least, played a significant role in his being one of the grantees of the town of Worcester. There were a few slaves and free men in the area, but most of today's Black citizens are descendants of migrants from the south. This explains the southern village atmosphere that I mentioned previously.

I have been blessed to be of a generation that has experienced significant changes. In the years preceding my mother's death, I had a love affair with Worcester, perhaps that's why I have never left. I can walk down the streets and remember when we used to ride the trolley all over the city for a dime.

Weekdays were pretty routine, but weekends were a time of adventure. There were piano, tap and baton lessons at the Lincoln Square Girls Club. Mrs. Barrett was my tap dancing teacher. There were walks up George Hill on Saturday mornings with Marilyn and her brother. They took piano lessons from Miss Grace Johnson Brown, the only Black piano teacher in the city.

On Sundays, there were walks to Bancroft Tower or to White City, the only amusement park in town. Sometimes we would walk back from White City and save our last dimes to buy double-decker ice cream cones.

Saturday afternoons frequently found us at a movie.

There were seven theaters. The best was the Loews Poli or the Palace, as it was called, and the worst was the Royal, with the Family running a close second. For a quarter we could go in and see the show as many times as we wished. The Plymouth was the only one that offered floorshows. The shows frequently featured Black artists and played on Sundays and Mondays. I saw some of the best on that stage: Peg Leg Bates, Cab Calloway and Nat King Cole. When I recall those years, I sometimes wish I had been old enough to grasp the importance of what I was seeing and hearing. The churches, the NAACP and other organizations sponsored concerts in Boston featuring Marian Anderson and Roland Hayes. Busloads of people would go to Boston for these events and when we arrived, the hail where the concerts were held were always as full as the buses.

When I was a bit older, I was allowed to attend the Baptist Young People's Union meetings at John Street Church. Our B.Y.P.U. attracted youngsters from all of the Black churches. Credit for that must be given to Hollister Guthridge, our leader. Hollister liked and understood young people. He allowed us to plan our own social events and run our meetings. But he always kept us in line and maintained discipline.

Those were puppy love days for most of the children. On warm summer nights boys and girls would walk home holding hands and discover love, stealing kisses in the shadows of the streetlights. I still thought that kissing boys was detrimental to one's health. But I was also the youngest in the group.

Another annual celebration that used to occur during my early childhood in Worcester *was* Emancipation Proclamation Day. Instead of celebrating in January, Worcester's Afro Americans joined with Boston, Springfield and Rhode Island to celebrate on the first of August. The celebration was sponsored by the Elks. On August 1st each year, a very large segment of Worcester's Black population boarded chartered buses and went to Crescent Park in Rhode Island. The Boston and Providence Elks Clubs also sponsored the excursion for the people in their areas. I remember it as a day of clam fritters, salt air, ice cream and dancing. There *was* always a band at the park's Ball Room. In later years after I became a woman, I saw a man killed in that ballroom. It was the last time that I ever went there.

Those were the days of my early childhood in. Worcester. When I returned to earn a living, many things had changed with both of us. I was rapidly becoming a woman.

For almost three years the job at Barrys went on, with me arguing for a raise and Feldman promising but never giving. Until early one fall Aaron, Feldman's son, began to come in more and more, and there would be two or three days when we wouldn't see the boss. One afternoon, Aaron, his face drawn and colorless, ran through the shop from the office and left without saying a word. An hour later, someone told us that Mr. Feldman had died. Within a month, Barry Sports Wear was out of business.

How long would I have continued to run a buck press if Mr. Feldman had lived? I honestly don't know. The fact was that I was running scared. Each day began with panic; my survival was my responsibility. My family was there for moral support but I had to clothe, feed and shelter myself. With this in mind, I hit the pavement once again looking for work. Only this time it was different, I had a trade. Or, so I thought. Starting at Park Avenue, and Chandler Street, I stopped at every tailor shop in sight. They all had buck presses but I was too dumb to figure out that they were not in mass production. In any event, I finally reached Portland Street and went into the last shop. By then my desperation must have been very visible. The shop's owner looked at me and shook his head to indicate that he did not need a buck press operator. Then the expression on his face signaled a great idea. He reached into a large cardboard box and came up with a handful of wire hangers. He instructed me to stand on the corner where I would get all of the people, going and coming, and as people passed I was to sell them hangers for a penny apiece. Needless to say, I didn't stay around long enough to discuss commission. To this day I believe he was sincerely trying to help me.

Meanwhile, independence had helped me develop a circle of friends. I met Jackie at church; she was younger than I was in years but in other ways, mature beyond her years. Jack and Jerry were cousins who came to Worcester from Roxbury to attend Worcester State Teachers College. They both graduated but I don't believe that either of them became teachers. Harry was a Worcester native who was the heart of our little group. He was the one that could be called on to act as escort if any of the girls wanted to attend an event and couldn't get a date. He tried to be all things to all people and usually wound up losing. This group would not be complete unless I mention Donald. He became my cousin Robbie's first husband. A Worcester native, Donald was a student at Holy Cross in those days, he never did graduate. You see how my peers may have influenced my decision to get on with my education.

Time was running out on me. I knew I had to get on with my plans, so I went to Commerce High and enrolled as a full-time student. When I explained what I was trying to do, the principal gave me permission to double up on courses. It was like coming home again and because so many World War II veterans were enrolled, I never felt out of place.

Somehow I managed to land a job at Cornell Dubilier. It

was a small shop located in one of the buildings behind the Union Station. Cornell manufactured radio transistors in all sizes. Well I'd always wanted a shot at piecework. Cornell Dubilier gave me my chance. The shop was staffed with women and supervised by a woman who, of course, reported to a man. The women sat at machines mounted on tables that very much resembled sewing machines. Each machine had a wheel and a spindle. To make transistors, the women simply had to precut strips of foil mounted on tissue paper, rolled it like a cigarette on the machine spindle and sealed it together with glue. You guessed it, no matter how hard I tried, I never made my quota.

Cornell's was unique in that it was not like most shops, nor were its employees the typical "shop women". The women who worked there were housewives who were working to help pay off a mortgage or educating their kids. They came to work dressed more like office clerks than shop women. They didn't curse or fight; in fact, the place was very peaceful. I enjoyed working there. My continued employment at Cornells can be credited to two people, the evening supervisor, Betty, and to my friend, Jessie, who more than once completed my order for me. On one occasion, Betty had to tell that she would be forced to let me go if I didn't make my quota. I think that she kept giving me a break because she could see how hard I was trying. Jessie, bless her heart, did everything in her power to teach me but in spite of her efforts, over half of my transistors came off the spindle crooked and useless.

Two blessings came from that job. The first was that it allowed me to be a full-time student. The second was that I met Jessie and through her the rest of her wonderful family. *Jessie* was a tall beautiful woman of African and American Indian descent. When she heard that I was looking for a room she told her parents, who invited me to their home to see a room that they had for rent.

Mr. and Mrs. Byard lived in a cozy little house on the corner of Carol and Liberty Streets. Since both of their sons and their daughter were married, they shared their home with Gramma (that's what everyone called her), Mrs. Byard's mother, and Trooper, the family's dog. The only way to describe the family is to say that they were kindness personified. When I arrived, after meeting everyone, I was invited into a large comfortable furnished front bedroom. It was a corner room with large windows that welcomed the sun. It had a double bed, an upholstered chair, a small desk and lamps. It was wonderful.

After all these years, trying to remember, trying to pull events into a tenable image, I stopped and cried for my Grandfather. I even said I love you aloud. If he had heard me, I wonder what his response would have been. We didn't have an opportunity to talk very often. The day that I told him that I had quit school was one of those rare times when we talked, alone together without saying what we really felt. In some ways Dad was more like Granddaddy than his other sons. He was a very sensitive man who had been hurt too often. On the day that I told him that I was going to quit school, we were in the barn, and he was working on something; he was always working on something. He didn't respond right away, when he did, he simply said, "I wish you'd stay in school, I wanted you to learn to push a pencil instead of a mop." couldn't look directly at him; if I had, I would never have gotten it said. My next statement was, "I'm going to get a job and save enough money to leave home and put myself through school." His reply was, "If that's what you want to do I can't stop you—you ought to finish school." Then I looked up and saw the tears in his eyes. He wept when his children died, he wept when his Arabian mare died and twice he wept for me.

When I told him that I had found a room and was leaving the farm he said "All right", nothing more. But his face had that strained expression that it sometimes had when he was hurt but felt that it would not be manly to show it.

My thirty-six Ford had gone the way of all old things and it had been replaced by a forty-one Ford. If the first was elegant, the latter was regal. It even sported a truck motor. It was that Ford that hauled me and my few belongings away from my grandfather's farm. I wanted so badly to hug him and tell him that everything would be all right, because it was time for me to go, I was eighteen years old. Instead I said good-bye and drove away knowing that I could never again return to that house to live. That summer with the Byards was one of the best that I have ever known. It was the first time in seven years that I felt free from the immediate threat of cruelty. Hannahbell had ceased to be physical but she had the sharp stinging tongue of a serpent.

I must explain that although I could not live with Momma and Granddaddy, they were there for me. They still provided advice and guidance. I spent many hours with them. We were family; there was never any doubt about that.

The Byards including Gramma were a wonderful family. Their house was a home that overflowed with gentleness and love for all living things. Gramma told me once how they came to have Trooper with them. It seems that one evening when they were sitting relaxing over their afternoon coffee, they heard a noise at the front door. When Mr. Byard investigated, he discovered a mongrel pup, bruised, battered and nearly starved. The family adopted him immediately. After feeding him and caring for his injuries, Mr. Byard named him

Trooper. He was an affectionate lovable mongrel but he could never tolerate the smell of liquor. If a stranger came in who smelled of it, Trooper would bristle. If someone that he knew smelled of liquor, he would stay away from them, this usually meant he would go to his corner in the kitchen.

The Byards and I had no trouble reaching an agreement. I paid one week in advance and planned to move in the following week. It was early spring. The first year back to school had gone smoothly, I felt good, I was on my way.

CHAPTER V

Worcester-Another Perspective

I SUPPOSE THAT every generation feels that the time of its youth was best. All things are enhanced in retrospect. Ours were the days of the big bands, romantic crooners and jazz quintets. There were three dance halls available to the Black community, Washburn in the Mechanics Hall building, AOH Hall on Trumbull Street and the Grand Army Hall on Pearl Street. For one dollar we could dance from eight until midnight to the music of a live band. When I say we, that usually meant Jackie and the others that I mentioned earlier. Everyone usually paid for his or her own ticket. That way, the girls didn't have to be concerned about whom they danced with. Dances were also held at Roseland Hall in Taunton, Lyonhurst in Marlboro and Sun Valley on Route 9. The really big bands played those locations. Dawn dances were frequently held at Roseland. We'd go to Taunton by bus, dance all night and ride home as the sun was rising. We were so exhilarated that the big orange disk rising above the horizon intensified the excitement. I used to go home, shower, change clothes, go to school and never begin to feel tired until the following evening. How strong we were.

It was during this time that I met a young man named Cornelius Spencer. Everyone called him Neak. That nickname is another story that I may tell one day. We met at a dance in Washburn Hall. Most Blacks have sort of black/brown hair, but not him. Neak's raven black hair was natural and beautiful with a satin luster. He had dimples then that danced around a little boy grin. He rarely presented a full smile and he was one of the few young men around who was taller that I was when I wore high heels. In addition, Spencer was one of the smoothest dancers in town. I believe that I can say that his cachets have always been, impeccably polished shoes and sparkling automobiles. Even when he wears jeans, his shoes must shine. In spite of the near misses that occurred in my life during the growing up process, I knew that I would eventually marry Neak Spencer. And so I did, almost ten years after we first met.

When I began to date a jazz pianist, I began to spend more time in Boston. That was the town; it offered places like Walleys Paradise, the Little Dixie, the Chicken Shack and the fabulous Hi Hat. All could be found on Columbus and Massachusetts Avenues. Let me not forget the Jazz Workshop where we spent so many Sunday afternoons. That jazz pianist was the first man that I almost married. He remains a very special person.

To be allowed into clubs one had to at least look 21. It helped to be tall. We brushed our hair into upsweeps, or combed it to one side. I frequently pulled mine back into a bun. We bought Parliament cigarettes. They matched the colors of the satin and crepe dresses clinging to our hips above the high heel shoes. We were so cool. I would feel so sophisticated at dances until the band played a slow drag and the only boy who asked me to dance had a konk. We would dance while the grease from his konkoleen hair mingled with his sweat to form a shiny circle on my powdered cheek.

The Negro clubs were children of segregation northern style. In the north integration only meant that white citizens could, if they wished, go slumming in Negro establishments and neighborhoods. However, it would not have been wise to reverse that situation. There have also been Negro entrepreneurs in Worcester for many years. The beauty parlors and barbershops were obvious. But, in addition, Clayton Street once featured Charlie Carlos' Pool Room. Directly in front of the Pool Room was Charlie Steel's shoeshine stand. Upet's store was on the corner of Laurel and Clayton. Upet (last name Hagopian) was one of the few white businesses on the street. The alley between Upets and the poolroom was where the men shot craps. One or two would always stand on the corner keeping an eye out for the police and women. Next to Upets was Mr. Lonnie Robert's fish market and the next building housed a variety of chicken coops and sandwich shops. Not all at the same time—one would open, go out of business and something else would take its place. In addition to these, Danny Brann and my grandfather had rubbish removal businesses and the Ward family had its chicken farm in Grafton. We also had professionals. In addition to three doctors, there were two lawyers, Attorneys Wallace and Dominus, musicians and several educators. What we did not have were enough people to provide strong financial support to our businesses and professionals.

Nowhere in the recorded histories of Worcester is there mention of the Quinsigamond Lodge No. 173 F.B.P.O. Elks of the World. Knowing of my interest in the history of Blacks in Worcester, a friend, Mr. James Walker, gave me one of the programs of the First Anniversary Reception and Ball of that organization held on Wednesday, January 4th, 1911. It is a lovely program printed by A. F. Hoyle of 419 Main Street. The first page is a greeting to welcome their guest and explain their purpose—Men banded together for the purpose of advancing the principals, which are based on the cardinal virtues of Charity, Justice, Brotherly Love and Fidelity. Page 2 features a picture of C. Sumner Mero, exalted Ruler and Founder. Page 3 is the concert program featuring the Cummins Full Orchestra of Boston. There was a march, an instrumental solo by Miss Grace Johnson, an Overture by the orchestra followed by Luigi Arditi's Love In Spring sung by Miss Mable Mero. Finally, Miss Ida M. Lewis of New York gave a reading.

What I like most is the menu:

Puree of Tomato with Crutons
Celery Olives
Broiled Salmon, Hollandaise Sauce—Green Peas
Escalloped Oysters Fritters Sultanna Sauce
Cold Sugar Cured Ham Ox Tongue
Roast Vermont Turkey, Cranberry Sauce
Mashed Potatoes Hubbard Squash
Lobster Salad, Mayonnaise Dressing
Assorted Cakes
Lemon Sherbet Holliquin Cream
American Cheese Boston Crackers
Demi Tasse
Supper 65 Cents T.A. Myers, Caterer

I couldn't believe how well everything was going. The school term couldn't have been better. In addition to their house on Carol Street, the Byards owned a cottage on Martha's Vineyard Island. They planned to move to the Island when they retired. Meanwhile, Mr. Byard, who was very talented, spent every weekend that he could fixing up the cottage. Since both Mr. and Mrs. Byard had serious problems with their eyes, neither of them could drive. So every weekend the Byards, Gramma, Trooper and I piled into my Ford and went to the Cape. At Buzzards Bay, all of us—the people, the car and the dog—boarded the ferry and sailed to Martha's Vineyard. What a wonderful summer.

Late that season, Cornell Dubilier announced its plans to close the Worcester shop and relocate in the South. Industries were seeking areas that provided lower taxes and cheap labor. I was out of work again; but this time there was no need to pound the pavement. Mrs. Byard ran an elevator at the Denholm and MacKay department store. Denholm's was looking for part-time operators, so naturally Mrs. Byard suggested that I apply. I did and I got the job.

Denholm's was an old establishment in an old building with old management. The elevators were the most antiquated items of all. They operated by a lever that came up out of the floor about 2 3/4 feet. At the end of the lever was a handle similar to the handle of a shovel. The operator griped the handle to move the lever *left* or right, left was down, right was up. This was done with the right hand. The left hand was *used* to open the heavy sliding metal doors. I hated Denholms. Each time I stepped into that metal cubicle, I became a human yo-yo. The tension of my string caused it to hum; "second floor, ladies lingerie, watch your step please." Rote, without thought; it was the most demeaning thing that I have ever done. A day's collection of dirt and sweat from hard work can leave one feeling fulfilled. That job left one stripped of dignity. The elevator operators were not only subservient to the customers; they were also second-class beings to the clerks, most of whom may have needed assistance just to find the place every morning. I probably should have turned around and walked out on the day that I started.

Things seemed to fall in place, including me. Late summer turned into fall and before long the Christmas holidays were approaching. I had developed a decent rapport with some of the employees; one of them was John, who was approximately my age. He was a college student working part—time and we just hit it off because of our ages and interests, certainly no more than that. He was blond with blue eyes and I was not. Toward the close of an exceptionally busy day, I had released a load of bodies on the ground floor and as I waited for more to get in, a woman stepped on. I can't remember what I was saying to John but I ended with something like, see you later. Then I pushed the lever and just as I did, my passenger said, "Get this damn thing up." I had never before known such a sudden wave of anger. It was as though all the humiliation of the previous months shot to the surface of my being like a buoy to the surface of an ocean. I literally threw the lever to the left, which sent the elevator crashing down to the ground floor. Then I turned and told the woman to get out.

Of course, the next day, before I got my uniform on, Mary, the store manager, called me to her office. I walked in and that woman was sitting there — false eyelashes, pancake make up and all. Mary didn't disappoint me, her first statement was a nauseatingly sweet, "Edna, I'm so surprised at you. Of all of our girls I never expected such a thing from you." I could feel the anger taking over again. For one thing, some of those "girls" were just as old as she was. Most of them were better people.

Then she said, "Apologize to Mrs. and I won't have to fire you." To which I replied, "You don't have to fire me, I quit".

There have been few events in my life that have made me feel so good inside.

My next venture was as a helper (cleaner of equipment) at the Louis Bregou Beauty Salon. It was a family business located upstairs over Eastons on the corner of Main and Pleasant Streets. It wasn't much of a job but the Bregous were a nice family and it was pleasant working for them. I probably would have remained there until graduation. However, late that spring Mr. Bregou went deep-sea fishing with some of his buddies. I believe that they capsized in a storm off the coast and Mr. Bregou drowned. His son, Fotis, ran the shop for a while but before long, he had to cut back and that meant that I was looking for work again.

Worcester is a unique city in many ways. More than its seven hills and ten colleges set it apart from cities similar in size. The city is spread out over a vast land area and is the second largest city in New England. Yet, through the years it has retained a small town atmosphere that, until recently, seemed unshakeable. Like a placid lake, it deceives the eye by camouflaging its strong undercurrents with a false sense of quiet. There have been advocates for social reform in Worcester since the days of the Underground Railroad. This article appeared in the Worcester Sunday Telegram on February 29, 1948:

> Among the ugliest pains inflicted by people upon each other is that caused by racial discrimination. It sears the soul. It is particularly foul because the person discriminated against has no control over his birth, race or color. It is foulest in the United States of America, which forbids discrimination in the constitution and Bill of Rights.

> For the past 13 years, a Worcester organization, not too well known, has been working steadily toward lessening racial prejudice The Inter-Racial Council of Worcester.[1]

Mr. Sandorf goes on to describe the Council's five-point program of objectives to implement and to achieve their goal of improving race relations. The Council was founded in December, 1934 as the Worcester Inter-Racial Friendship Groups. It was first suggested by Mrs. Paul G. Macey. Among the charter members were Miss Elizabeth Craighead, a Commerce High French teacher, Mrs. Carl D. Skillin, Mrs. Grace Johnson Brown, a black music teacher, Mrs. Russell 0. Quinton and Mrs. Hollis W. Coff.

On May 14, 1943, five years after I arrived in Worcester, the Council came out of the closet and held its first public meeting in the Friendship Room of the Worcester Federal Savings and Loan Association. recall attending their Roland Hayes concert given in Atwood Hall in May, 1947. At that time, Reverend Marvin Gibson, pastor of John Street Baptist Church, served on the Executive Committee. John S. Laws and Mrs. Joseph H. Brevard, both black educators, were active in the Council.

Many people were involved but one name stood out above the others to become synonymous with social justice in the city of Worcester. That was Mrs. Juanita M. Farber. Mrs. Farber's name became a household word in the Black community.

She *was* president of the Interracial Council for 19 years and seemed to have a personal vendetta against racism. She

1 Ivan Sandorf, Worcester Sunday Telegram, February 29, 1948, P.2.

made herself available to the community on what appeared to be a twenty-four hour basis. In *times* of trouble, Mrs. Farber helped families acquire lawyers or raise *bail* in some instances. Born in Grand Rivers, Kentucky, she waged her noblest battles in Worcester. Mrs. Farber is credited with the hiring of the first black sales clerks in Worcester stores and I am sure that she and the Council assisted Mr. Bartlett in securing an employment interview for me at the State Mutual Life Assurance Company in 1956, although I never had the pleasure of meeting her.

Before her death on Tuesday, January 3, 1978, Mrs. Farber was the recipient of the Harry Smith Oswell Award from the National Association for the Advancement of Colored People, the 1950 American Veterans Committee Freedom Award, a special award issued from the Worcester Housing Authority for her work after the tornado of 1953 and a citation of merit from the United Negro College Fund, National Conference of Christians and Jews and the Massachusetts House of Representatives for her work at Friendly House.

No study of the history of blacks in Worcester would be complete without mentioning Mrs. Farber. It took a special kind of courage for her and others like her to take a stand before it became socially acceptable to do so.

The actions of the Council started many changes. The first Black policeman, Errol Hawley, was hired in 1948. The following year, George Spence, "the gentle giant", joined the force. George was at least six feet five, a big guy without a violent bone in his body. Louis Shropshire, Jr. joined the force in 1954. The only way to describe him is to say that he is a Black Gentleman Jim. These appointments were a start. Things were slowly and painfully changing.

The weather report for Sunday, April 24, 1955 was cloudy,

cool, showers. Monday: cloudy. Three quarters of an inch high letters screamed out, under the date and twenty cents: "Beeliner Kills Man At Jamesville Station". In smaller letters, "Robert Jarrett, 86, was walking tracks". A picture was there with a Celtic cross to mark the spot on the track where his mangled body landed at 7:30 p.m. on Saturday, April 23, 1955. The body could not be embalmed so they put him in a white linen bag and closed the glass top coffin. In his obituary they called him the Reverend Robert Jarrett. Granddaddy would have liked that.

Again, I found a job; this time as a "go for" at the Bushong Photography studio, another family business. The entire Bushong family is talented. Polly ran the studio and the eldest brother worked with her. Polly Bushong is a totally sensitive, feeling woman. To this day, I believe that she gave me the job out of the kindness of her heart. She certainly didn't need me. Not only did she keep me on her payroll until I graduated, she was also our class photographer and she gave me my graduation pictures. I would not have had them otherwise.

CHAPTER VI

The Final Isolation

I DON'T REMEMBER what I wore on that morning in May 1956. If I owned a suit, I suppose that was it and, of course, white gloves. We were taught that a suit with a white blouse and white gloves were the standard uniform for employment interviews. I remember walking down Walnut Street to the State Mutual Building.

Priscilla Peterson interviewed me and asked all of the ridiculous questions that they used to ask in those days. Do you have a boy friend? Do you have marriage plans, etc.? After Priscilla, I was interviewed by Frank Killion, Manager of the Group Accounts Department. Somehow I knew, without being told, that I had landed the job. When the phone call came the next day and Mr. Bartlett told me the news I was elated. I went back to State Mutual so that Priscilla could tell me what my *new* job would be and that I would earn $40.00 per week. I couldn't stay calm any longer. I left State Mutual and called everyone that I could think of to tell them the good news.

With a clearly defined goal I entered State Mutual for what was going to be no more than two years. During that time, I would save enough money to permit me to enter college as a full-time student. Then I would work part-time or evenings. I stopped worrying about work, because somehow I always seemed to find a job when I needed one. By the way, I had decided to major in English, having discovered Edna St. Vincent Millay. I believe it was her first name that got me; in addition to her work.

Jackie had worked at State Mutual for about a month before I made the scene. However, I'm sure that only her department head, supervisor and the Personnel Department knew that she was black. Until this day I'm sure that some of the people who worked with her still don't know. Then along came Thompson, all five feet seven of her; a big fly in a medium size bowl of buttermilk. For all practical purposes, I was the only brown bomber in town. The two-way education began. In all fairness to my Company and I say that with fondness, I would not have remained if the rewards had not outweighed the hardships. Some marvelous people have left their marks on this Company and I have been blessed to have known many of them. There is a phenomenon connected with being black and/or different in any society. I say any society rather than America, because I have experienced it in England and other European countries. The phenomenon is that whenever you enter an area, whether it is a building or street, where the societal majority is in the majority, you become the focus of their attention. This can be unnerving for the very young, because it is almost as though the so-called majority is trying to stare you away. One learns to project a facade of coolness but one never gets used to it. Perhaps that's because it's a reminder of how vulnerable we always are.

The Group Insurance Operations was like a company within a company. As insurance goes, it was a relatively new venture, the brainchild of H. Ladd Plumley who was the company president in 1956. It wasn't until a few years later that he was named Chairman of the Board and Chief Executive Officer.

There are very few things about my first day at State Mutual that I remember. A welcome chat with Frank Killion in his office, introductions to Ken Long and Jack Durning and finally I was turned over to my supervisor, Martha Pashoian. Martha shared that status with Gladys Forrest, a lovely lady. Muzzie (nick name) was the senior clerk responsible for checking my work and the work of three other clerks.

Each senior clerk was responsible for checking the work of four junior clerks. Obviously, I had to be matched up with a team that *was* willing to accept me. Someone outdid himself; my team couldn't have been better. I will never forget their consideration and obvious efforts to understand.

Given the right scenario, even an individual who never accepted, believed or lived the stereotype will expend a great deal of energy trying to be small and inconspicuous. How foolish I was. I can remember filing group cards on my first day and not wanting to make any noise. I filed some in the top drawer, pushed the drawer halfway in, then began to file in the bottom drawer. When I finished filing the last cards and stood up, my head came up directly under the top drawer with a loud crash that sounded like a bomb exploding in a cannon. Every eye on the floor seemed to turn in my direction.

There were others in the Company and in Group Operations who weren't as willing to adapt to my presence as my team was. It must be said for the shop women that I have worked with that the overwhelming majority of them were clean, honest people, black and white. Their confrontations were direct face-to-face actions like, "Honey, give your soul to Jesus 'cause your ass belongs to me". That was the favorite expression of one particular woman. It's not afternoon tea conversation but it is an honest face-to-face challenge. I am eternally grateful that I never had any problems. I developed a quick smile and inherited a phenomenal flee reflex.

Yet there have been times through the years when I would have paid a good price for an honest face-to-face exchange. Instead, the word nigger or niggardly would be used casually in cafeteria line conversation. Another favorite was "Let's call a spade a spade." There were a few budding young managers who *were* determined to get me out of "their" company. When they pulled their stunts, they would make a point of standing as close as possible to me and after their comment, they would stare at me waiting for the explosion. It never came, I was determined to survive. No one was going to force me out. I used to feel the hair on the back of my neck bristle but I learned that people like that cannot bear to be ignored. I learned to use that. I also learned that most of the sophisticated office employees were sadly lacking in confidence.

Many of those who spoke and smiled in the building almost ran head on into traffic to avoid speaking on the street. Shop women don't seem to have that problem. They know who they are. Until this day, I never speak to a fellow employee when I meet one away from the office, unless he or she speaks first. I don't have time to play games and I've known my identity for years. The amusing part of this is that now my eyes are failing and I don't always see people. This has put me in hot water a few times.

As time progressed, I learned to stop trying to be inconspicuous and decided to let my obvious high visibility work for me. I began to bounce through those hallowed halls with a big smile and a "Hi!" for everyone that I met in the corridors, even the confirmed bigots. How well we learn to wear our masks. Part of this facade included not getting hung up on names. That proved to be a mistake. It's like designating everyone an enemy. Nothing could be further from the truth. If that were so, I would never have survived. Nevertheless, I took that route, it became a habit and to this day, I have difficulty remembering who's who at the office. The exceptions to this, of course, are the people that I work with on a daily basis. One gentleman was especially polite and always smiled and spoke wherever I saw him in the building. I learned later that he was Mr. Plumley. I will always have the very highest regards for Plumley. Another gentleman that I admire is Mr. Jack Adam, retired president of The Hanover Insurance and Worcester Mutual Companies.

In spite of the obstacles, I enjoyed my work and I enjoyed my association with the majority of my fellow workers. I did have to fight for every inch of progress that I made but that was to my advantage, it made me stronger. Society shapes us all to the extent that at times we cannot differentiate right from wrong. I have always had to turn out twice as much work and be twice as good just to survive. But I also know that some of those who did not want to pay me as much as they paid the white clerks just couldn't understand the wrong of it. I talked to one of my managers and he was truly surprised to learn that I had dreams and aspirations that I wanted many of the same things that his other employees wanted.

State Mutual and I have done a lot of growing together. In 1957, we moved into the beautiful new building on Lincoln Street. I was a problem to management. The procedure that they followed was to promote from within the unit as employees terminated. When our senior clerk left due to pregnancy, Slim moved up into her slot. If I haven't mentioned it, Slim was one of the best friends that I ever had. When Slim married and became pregnant something had to be done with me. I was more than capable of doing anything that had to be done in my unit and had the ability to learn any job in the department. The problem was that although the white women weren't treated on an equal basis with the white men, they were at least held in too high an esteem to ask them to work for a Negro.

To solve this problem, a job was made for me. I was given all of the special accounts cases, twice the work, half the pay. By now the heat of battle had warped my senses. I was determined to "make it" at State Mutual. I would never let bigots force me out. I just had to think of another way to reach my goal.

Meanwhile, I also got married and became pregnant. In those days, pregnant women wore smocks and skirts. What we did was pass them back and forth. Jackie had left the Company a year or so after her employment and she had already had her first child. There was my maternity wardrobe except for skirts; she was no more than five feet five. The old maternity skirts used to have a hole in the front for your belly with a T string effect that was attached by a drawstring at the waist. I never did get big enough to fill up my skirts but that didn't matter to me, just being pregnant made me feel beautiful all over. One of those days when I was wearing my favorite black and white smock and feeling very pleased with myself I was working at one of the file drawers in the middle of the floor and, as I worked, my skirt very slowly crept down and before I realized what was happening, it lay in a heap around my ankles. It was one of the best laughs that some of us had experienced in a while. I had learned to laugh at myself.

In 1958 there was no such thing as maternity leave. One's employment was terminated instead. On Friday, November

8, 1958, I went home feeling great. I washed my kitchen floor, did some laundry and a few other things. My employment terminated on that date; but not for long. The country experienced a brief recession in 1958 and it hit us hard. My husband was laid off by the foundry and couldn't find a job anywhere. He finally wound up packing apples for Rudnick and Maher. It was something to do but certainly not adequate to support a family. We were both determined that our beautiful baby would have the best of everything. She was beautiful, the most beautiful little thing that I have ever seen. When Dad came by to see his great-granddaughter, he held her and beamed all over. I wish that they could have spent more time together. Anyway, the only solution to our financial problems was for me to go back to State Mutual. It was rough. I was breast-feeding and my baby was less than eight weeks old. I did not want to leave her. If I had it to do again, I would take a different route. For a second time State Mutual found me at its door. Again, I talked to Priscilla who once again gave me the old routine before calling me the following day to go to work. I have been working ever since.

For about fifteen months I worked in the Group Operations until, one day in the sixties a department store cleaning lady, Mrs. Rosa Parks, told Blacks to stop sitting in the backs of buses and Doctor King assured us that we could overcome. The Black Revolution had begun. Civil Rights legislation began to be passed; companies found themselves in a position of having to meet quotas. I emphasize the word quotas because, unfortunately, a large portion of this country's management thinks in quotas rather than ethics. Clever managers grabbed the first warm black body that they could find and put it in the most conspicuous spot, the Personnel Department. I was it for State Mutual. As the years progressed this proved to be a cruel process. Some blacks found themselves suddenly placed in management positions that they had not *been* properly prepared to handle. Most learned the ropes and survived but there were others who failed. Such a failure is very difficult to deal with because it can cause its victims to begin to accept and live the stereotype.

Programmed by the events of my life to survive, I entered the Personnel Department determined to learn everything that I possibly could. No job, as long as it was honest, was too difficult or insignificant for me to tackle. I didn't know that this was where I would have some of the best and some of the worst of my professional experience.

I stated previously that I have met and worked with many fine people at State Mutual. It would take a second book for me to list and comment about all of them. However, there are two that I must at least mention. One is my friend, Pearl Evans. Or, Pretty Pearl, as my husband calls her. She also started her State Mutual career in the Group Operations. She is a lovely lady, with prematurely silver hair that frames her face with soft natural waves. And, as if that weren't enough, she has dancing blue eyes. At one time or another, it seemed that the majority of the men in the Company have had a crush on Pearl. Her physical beauty is secondary to the internal goodness of the woman. She and her husband, Russell, will always be special to me. Another friend is Kitty Stevens. Born in Billings, Montana, Kitty saw her first Black man when she was nineteen years old. She boarded a train to come east and marry a handsome sailor that she'd met named Edward Stevens. She and I have had many belly laughs in the Bullock Hall cafeteria, especially when we compared our childhood experiences. And more than once we have been fascinated by the many similarities of the experiences of the white child on a ranch in Billings, Montana, and a black child on a farm in Oakridge, Tennessee.

For the first year in the Personnel Department I did my usual double share, but the supervisor never got over being forced to work with a Negro, she downgraded my appraisal form and refused to recommend me for a raise. Even though the Personnel Director admitted to me that she was wrong, he refused to reverse her decision. After a few tears, I became even more determined to learn all that I could learn about personnel work. My first promotion with State Mutual was to the position of Supervisor of Personnel Administration. I have spent most of my career with the Company in the Personnel Department, advancing from clerk to supervisor, to administrator and finally to Assistant Manager.

Meanwhile the politics and the opposition never stopped. Before becoming supervisor I was offered a job as secretary to one of the men in the Administrative Operations who had recently been promoted to the level of Vice President. I didn't want the job and thank God he didn't want me. When he came into Personnel and the interviewer told him that she suggested me for the job, he looked at me with the kind of hatred that distorts the human face and gives it the appearance of a rabid animal. Today, he smiles and speaks and so do I but we both know what he is.

When I first moved to Personnel, a vice president of our affiliate called and cursed at me over the phone, he wasn't even man enough to face me. Needless to say that one went all the way up to the President's office and I received an apology. One of my most ticklish experiences occurred when a personnel head tried to make me the scapegoat for an error that he had made. Having learned many years before to keep my C.Y.A. (cover your ass) file in order, there was no way that

I could let that happen. The trick was never to call the liar a liar; that's insubordination. What I did instead was verify to everyone concerned my part in the procedure and since my part of the transaction was correct, that left him to deal with the rest. He retired early.

One learns to deal with every situation. When State Mutual was planning to move its largest affiliate to Worcester, the Personnel staff had to work with The Hanover Personnel people to arrange to transfer records. My first business trip was to The Hanover Office in New York to help get the move lined up. Everything went well until the two women from the New York office came to Worcester. Hanover invited its key people to Worcester in the hope of convincing them to move to Worcester with the Company. My assignment was to entertain the women while they were here. One evening I was assigned to take them and the benefits clerk out to dinner. We decided to have dinner at a new place on West Boylston Street. We went to our table, ordered our meals and kept the usual uncomfortable, trying to be friendly, conversation going. To this day, I don't know what we were talking about, the only thing that I remember is that the benefits clerk, after having a couple of drinks for courage, said, "What do you think we are, niggers like you?" Later, I told my husband that I never came so close to smashing someone with a duck. I had ordered duck for dinner. However, years of training paid off, in her case it was bigotry blended with petty jealousy. Sixty years of living hadn't taught her a thing. Before the evening was over, she looked like, and *she* must have felt like, a complete fool.

Life is a glorious adventure and a constant challenge to those who are willing to accept it. I think of all that has happened in my life. Most of those who were near and dear to me as a child are gone. Clara, Robbie and I are all that is left of our family who were part of the great migration. One day in her one hundred and seventh year, Momma lay down to take an afternoon nap and went to be with Granddaddy. Their sons, Hugh, Robert Lee, Williard, Frank and Ted all died within a six year period. My sweet Ben died when he was just a boy, a country boy who just hadn't learned how to deal with city folks. As for Hannahbell of the beautiful feet and legs, she spends her days in a wheelchair, having lost both of her legs to diabetes.

There have been supporters where and when I least expected it. I have learned that I can never afford to forget, or to become color blind in the corporate community. Least I forget, there is always someone to remind me, like the department director who did not agree with the procedure used to bill him for a CLU examination that he failed. He wrote a memo to my boss concerning me, it didn't matter that I didn't make the rules. I think he was bothered by the fact that I knew that he simply didn't have the ability to pass the examinations. The subject of his memo was "One On The Blackhand Side". So the battle never ends.

Yet, when I leave State Mutual there will be waves of nostalgia for me as there are for others. I started as a child and progressed through a psychological adolescence at about thirty-five.

My goal was to earn a college degree. My experience has been one of growth and fulfillment.

In 1973 I realized that it was time for me to make a serious effort to reach my goal. I began by enrolling in the Evening College of the Quinsigamond Community College. I graduated in 1976 with honors, receiving an Associate Degree in Business Administration. That same year I decided to take advantage of the Clark University Family Plan. My husband had worked at Clark for several years. In 1980 I graduated cum laude from the University, receiving a Bachelor of Science Degree in Liberal Arts. This work is my Master's thesis, and it will be submitted to the faculty of Clark University. As I complete this work, I remember the heartbreak of having to quit high school, and thank God for my determination to return.

Success has many yardsticks. This is a very small portion of the best of how I have lived. June Jordan, in her essay for *A Celebration of Black Women*, wrote, "The work of our mothers too often never won victories of any-kind-except the potential for a completely different kind of work for us." Sometimes I sit in my air-conditioned, carpeted office and remember Oakridge. Love is the same, the woman has changed, the isolation never ends.

We are genetically programmed to survive. Our genes seem to have been projected on this survival course without choice. This is why we are all here. Not one of us put himself or herself here. As human animals became more human (not necessarily more humane) and gained sufficient affluence, the number of choices increased. When faced with a variety of choices, we are confronted with the problem of establishing priorities. Determining the order of priorities is the turning point for both individuals and societies.

Ivan Hill, Common Sense And Everyday Ethics.
Hand Book, The Ethics Resource Center,
Washington, D.C., 1980, P.23.

Bibliography

Books

Bunch, Ralph J. The Political Status of the Negro In The Age of FDR. Chicago: The University of Chicago Press, 1973.

Cade, Tone The Black Woman: An Anthology. New York: The New American Library, Inc., 1970.

Davidson, Don The Tennessee Valley. New York: Toronto Rhinehart & Co., Inc., 1946.

Erskine, Margaret H. Worcester: An Illustrated' History. Woodland Hills, Cal.: Windsor Publications, Inc., 1981.

Folmsbee, S. J., Cortew, R. E., & Mitchell, E. L. Tennessee: A Short History. Knoxville: The University of Tennessee Press, 1969.

Franklin, John H. From Slavery To Freedom. New York: Vintage Books, 1969.

Hare, Nathen & Hare, Julia Soul-Black Experience. New York: Transaction Books, 1970.

Johnson, Charles W. & Jackson, Charles O. City Behind A Fence. Knoxville: The University of Tennessee Press, 1981.

Johnson, D. M. & Campbell, R. R. Black Migration In America. Durham, N.C.: Duke University Press, 1981.

Lamon, Lester C. Blacks In Tennessee 1791-1970. Knoxville: The University of Tennessee Press, 1981.

Lincoln, C. Eric The Negro Pilgrimage In America. New York: Bantam Books, Inc., 1967.

Martin, E. P. & Martin, J. M. The Black Extended Family. Chicago: The University of Chicago Press, 1978.

Nelson, John Worcester County, A Narrative History Vol. II. New York: The American Historical Society, Inc., 1934.

Nutt, Charles History of Worcester and Its People Vol. I. New York: *Lewis* Historical Publishing Co., 1919.

Odum, Howard W. Rainbow Round My Shoulder. Indianapolis: The Bobbs-Merrill Co., 1928.

Redding, J. Saunders On Being Negro In America. Howard W. Sams & Co., Inc., 1951-62.

Stack, Carol B. All Our Kin. New York: Harper Inc., 1974

Willie, Charles V. A New Look At Black Families. Bayside, N.Y., General Hall, Inc., 1981.

Willie, Charles V. The Family Life of Black People. Ohio: Charles E. Merrill. Publishing Co., 1970.

Theses

Grant, Nancy, "Blacks, Regional Planning and the TVA". (Ph.D. dissertation, University of Chicago, 1978)

Reports

N.A.A. C.P. Proceedings of 1955 Annual Meeting. New York: 1955.

Work Projects Administration For the State of Tennessee, Tennessee: The American Guide. New York: Hastings House, 1939.

Newspapers

"Beeliner Kills Man At Jamesville Station", Worcester Sunday Telegram. April 24, 1955. Section A P.1.

"Improving Race Relations, Worcester Sunday Telegram. February 29, 1948. Feature Parade Section 1)5,

"Juanita Farber, Was Social Worker", Worcester Evening Gazette. January 4, 1978. Obituary P.10.

CPSIA information can be obtained at www.ICGtesting.com
Printed in the USA
BVOW072253010812

296831BV00001B/80/P